CONCILIUM

CONCILIUM/VOL. 30

SCRIPTURE

HOW DOES THE CHRISTIAN CONFRONT THE OLD TESTAMENT?

edited by PIERRE BENOIT, O.P.
ROLAND E. MURPHY, O. CARM.
BASTIAAN VAN IERSEL, S.M.M.

VOLUME 30

CONCILIUM
theology in the age of renewal

PAULIST PRESS
NEW YORK, N.Y. / GLEN ROCK, N.J.

The Imprimatur for this volume applies
only to articles by Roman Catholic authors.

NIHIL OBSTAT: John E. Brooks, S.J., S.T.D.
                                    Censor Deputatus

IMPRIMATUR: ✠ Bernard J. Flanagan, D.D.
                                Bishop of Worcester

November 24, 1967

The Nihil Obstat and Imprimatur are official declarations that a book or
pamphlet is free of doctrinal or moral error. No implication is contained
therein that those who have granted the Nihil Obstat and Imprimatur agree
with the contents, opinions or statements expressed.

Library of Congress Catalog Card Number: 67-31633

Suggested Decimal Classification: 291.8

Paulist Press assumes responsibility for the accuracy of the English translations in this Volume.

PAULIST PRESS
EXECUTIVE OFFICES: 304 W. 58th Street, New York, N.Y. and 21 Harris-
    town Road, Glen Rock, N.J.
Executive Publisher: John A. Carr, C.S.P.
Executive Manager: Alvin A. Illig, C.S.P.
Asst. Executive Manager: Thomas E. Comber, C.S.P.

EDITORIAL OFFICES: 304 W. 58th Street, New York, N.Y.
Editor: Kevin A. Lynch, C.S.P.
Managing Editor: Urban P. Intondi

Printed and bound in the United States of America by
The Colonial Press Inc., Clinton, Mass.

CONTENTS

PART II

BIBLIOGRAPHICAL SURVEY

PART III

DOCUMENTATION CONCILIUM
Office of the Executive Secretary
Nijmegen, Netherlands

Preface

Pierre Benoit, O.P./*Jerusalem, Jordan*

Roland E. Murphy, O. Carm./*Washington, D.C.*

Bastiaan van Iersel, S.M.M./*Nijmegen, Netherlands*

The 1966 Scripture volume of *Concilium* (Vol. 20) exemplified the dynamics of biblical tradition within both the Hebrew and the Christian Bible. The ongoing life of the Word within the People of God produced reinterpretation and additions within the Word itself. Thus the intimacy between Bible and community was etched into the biblical text. In this issue the Bible and the community again come together—specifically: How does the Christian confront the Hebrew Bible, which he terms the "Old Testament"? This question is a perennial one —in one age Marcion replied by eliminating the Hebrew Bible; in another Augustine wrote the massive dictum that dominated Christian exegesis of the Old Testament for so many years: the New Testament is hidden in the Old, and the Old Testament is made plain in the New. The fact is that the style in which the Church confronts the Hebrew Bible varies in every age. And this is only right; the needs of the times color one's correlation of the Old with the New.

With the advent of the rigorous historical approach to ancient literature, a more adequate understanding of the Hebrew Bible *on its own terms* has been reached. And the Christian must hear the Word on this level, or he will hopelessly flatten out the divine message. Thus, from his prison Dietrich Bonhoeffer wrote of the strong influence which his reading of the Old Testament was hav-

1

ing on him—that it was not really Christian to want to get to the New Testament too soon and too directly. On the other hand, the Christian believes that Christ is the fulfillment of Israel's hope; he lives by the spirit of fulfillment of the Scriptures echoed in the pages of the New Testament. The essays in this volume of *Concilium* illustrate several approaches to this question.

John L. McKenzie writes of the enduring values of the Hebrew Bible, as these can be seen against the background of the ancient Near East, and as they can be oriented to Christian self-understanding. His emphasis on the existential aspect of the Word is continued in the study of F. Dreyfus. Franco Festorazzi explores the salvific experience of faith as it emerges from the Old Testament into the New. J. G. Vink examines certain constants and variables in both Testaments. Elpidius Pax enters into the problem of the law and commandments, especially in the light of Christ's fulfillment. Heinrich Gross analyzes the relationship between royal messianism and the eschatological hope of Israel, and he gives an open-ended perspective to the figures of the Servant and the Son of Man. Salvador Muñoz Iglesias looks for the perfection which the Christian revelation brings to the Israelite experience as this developed from promise to fulfillment. Hilaire Duesberg attempts to view the Old Testament from a distinctly Christian point of view, with particular emphasis on the Psalms.

The hermeneutical problem in recent Catholic literature has emerged in terms of the fuller sense (*sensus plenior*). One of the foremost exponents of this theory, Joseph Coppens, presents the current state of the question in the bibliographical survey.

These essays could not even hope to be exhaustive. But they may stand as guidelines for the ever fruitful encounter of the Christian with the Hebrew Bible.

PART I
ARTICLES

John L. McKenzie, S.J./*Notre Dame, Indiana*

The Values of the Old Testament

The Christian faithful have themselves raised the question of the values of the Old Testament in specific terms. This generation has seen a revival of interest in the Old Testament which has had no parallel in the Church for several hundred years, if indeed it has ever had a parallel. The faithful have professed their belief that the Old Testament ought to have values for the contemporary Christian; they have eagerly sought these values, asked their clergy and their biblical scholars to point them out, and expressed dissatisfaction when these values were not clearly presented. The renewal of the Church, which began before the Second Vatican Council was strongly biblical in tone, and it quickly became apparent that the Christian Bible is not limited to the New Testament. The more interested one becomes in the New Testament, the more clearly one perceives that the New Testament is the second part of a book. What is to be done with the first part?

In spite of some excellent work done by scholars during the last twenty years, the question of the values of the Old Testament is not yet fully answered. Were it fully answered, an article of this sort would not be requested. The purpose of this article cannot be to set forth the values of the Old Testament fully and finally. The article must of necessity reflect the personal interest and personal endeavors of the author; this does not mean that

5

the author can afford to be unacquainted with the work of others. But it is just in this area of "values" that personal judgment enters in vigor. One can do no more than set forth those values which seem to him to be most pertinent, to advert to the work of his colleagues, and to attempt to set forth a programmatic outline which must be filled in by further exposition.[1]

The Christian faithful seek specifically Christian values in the Old Testament. Christians have sought these since New Testament times, and they have sought them in a number of diverse ways. Many of these ways, acceptable to Christians of earlier times, are not acceptable in modern times. Thus the discovery of accurate predictions of New Testament persons, incidents and institutions can no longer be sustained. The allegorical interpretation which sought a hidden Christian meaning beneath the surface of the letter likewise can no longer be sustained. Modern scholarship has been quicker to show that these older methods are not valid than it has been to point out other values. Thus biblical criticism sometimes appears to have left a vacuum precisely in the area of the Christian values of the Old Testament. The fact that these older methods really did not make most of the Old Testament meaningful is sometimes not noticed. The Old Testament is the Bible of the Jews; obviously they find in it values that Christians do not expect to share. Yet the search continues; it is not discouraged by the uncertainty which modern scholarship has often shown in presenting the Old Testament to the Christian Church as a book of the Church. To present the Old Testament in this way must be the ultimate purpose of this article.

[1] Two important recent works which deal with our topic must be mentioned: P. Grelot, *Sens chrétien de l'Ancien Testament* (Paris, 1962); C. Larcher, *L'actualité chrétienne de l'Ancien Testament* (Paris, 1962).

I

Universal Values

Before we approach the specifically Christian values of the Old Testament, it seems wise to consider some values that are not specifically Christian. While the Old Testament is the book of the Church, it is not the exclusive property of the Church; anyone who wishes may buy a copy and read it. It is, as we have noticed, the Bible of the Jews. In the last century before the Christian era we find that Jewish intellectuals attempted to present their Scriptures to the Hellenistic world as a book that contained all that was best in Greek thought without the basic errors that these apologists pointed out in Greek thought. The Old Testament belongs to world literature, along with Homer, Dante and Shakespeare. It is impossible to think of any scheme of education that could pretend to be education and fail to introduce its students to the Old Testament. One can consider the Old Testament as literature and history, as a record of human achievement and human failure and a monument to the human genius of expression without giving any religious assent to the Old Testament. The student who approaches the books with a neutral attitude or even with a hostile attitude can be expected to find some values in it. What may these values be?

The basic error that ancient Jewish apologists found in Greek thought was the error of polytheism; they gave it the simplistic name of idolatry, although Greeks were not idolaters, and in fact the greatest Greek thinkers paid little or no allegiance to Greek religion of classical mythology. The apologists claimed that their sacred books set forth clearly and convincingly that idea for which Greek philosophers unsuccessfully strove: the idea of one God, monotheism. They could have added that their books presented one God who was genuinely personal. They overstated this value; the God of the Old Testament, although one in number, was no easier for Greek philosophical thought to assimilate than were the gods of mythological polytheism. But they were surely right in claiming that their monotheistic faith left no room for gross superstition; and the history of Judaism vindicates this claim, for even in areas where Jewish belief and practice showed some strange deviations, Judaism as a whole has always rejected superstition. In this respect it has been and is as rationalist as one could desire. Here Judaism has been the faithful heir of the Law, the prophets and the wise men. If the Old Testament is ranked with the great world literature that searches God, it must be admitted that it searches for God and not for something less.

World literature survives and becomes classic not so much because it searches God but because of its insight into man and the human condition. The student finds these insights in the Old Testament in forms they do not have in other ancient literature. In two respects the Old Testament has a breadth of vision not equalled in other ancient classics: its sense of man as man and its sense of man in history. The first of these claims could occasion some surprise; it would be easy to cite passages that are narrow, tribal or nationalistic and xenophobic. One need think only of the Israelite attitude toward the Canaanites, of the cries of vengeance against Babylon and Edom, and of certain less agreeable aspects of the consciousness of election. But a classic shows man when he is small as well as when he is great. The same collection, which is at times narrow and tribal, also looks to the union of all men in the worship of one God. It sees the old idea of tribal community becoming worldwide. It sees man in his origins as a single group, and the dispersion of men into nations as the result of sinful pride. It sees one moral standard for all peoples. One finds in Job an insight into the common and universal experience of suffering that is one of the most precious items in all literature. The modern reader, whether he is a believer or not, may be offended by the narrowness and miss the spaciousness. He should be aware of the utter absence of any humane spaciousness in the literature of Egypt and Mesopotamia, and the thoughtless arrogance with which the Greeks divided the world into Greeks and barbarians; then he may come to understand that much of his humanitarian breadth has its roots in the Old Testament. He may also begin to wonder whether his humanitarianism is as broad as he thinks it is.

There is no parallel whatever in ancient literature, even in Greek historians, to the Old Testament vision of man in history; and the biblical idea of history is at the root of the modern idea of history, particularly in history viewed as evolution. The Old Testament sees man, we have noticed, as a single group; it also sees the human adventure as a single experience. Both of these unities are formed on the Israelite belief in one God. The Old Testament idea of man in history is in no way secular. God originated history, and God will bring history to a term. Everything that happens falls under his sovereignty. The Old Testament does not avoid the speculative danger of determinism; it is rather serenely unaware of it. The history of man is a history of man's actions, and man is a responsible agent. His actions fall under the judgment of God, which is accomplished in history. The key to the unity of history is the idea of the sovereignty or the "reign" of God, toward which history moves. In each crisis of history God asserts his sovereignty ever more explicitly. The historical and geographical horizons of the Old Testament were limited, but the principle of the unity of history does not suffer from these limitations.

We have noticed that the Old Testament does not attend to the problem of determinism. Here it stands in striking contrast with most of Greek thought, which was haunted by the inability of man to overcome destiny. The Greek specter of destiny broods over the scene both in religious and secular Greek writers; it creates a mood of pessimism that is the antithesis of the Greek joy of life. The Old Testament confronted with man in history can hardly be called either pessimistic or optimistic; in spite of its confession of divine sovereignty, man's history is what man makes it to be. The Old Testament shows no less joy in life than Greek literature shows. What takes the joy out of life, when it goes, is not irrational destiny but sin. Man in history is never in the Old Testament a helpless victim. Whatever happens to man is rational; and this is perhaps the finest form of optimism. The expressions of the optimism at times may be too simple for modern readers; they were too simple for the author of Job. But Job did not think of solving the problem by denying that human history is basically rational. Had the problem of destiny been proposed to the Israelites, they would have called it a form of superstition. The Old Testament is a document of the inner freedom of man.

The ideal of freedom must be set in a context of other ideas, and first in the context of God's sovereignty. This sovereignty is asserted in the Old Testament in God's saving and judging acts. God's sovereignty does not permit him to be governed by the acts of man; the saving and judging acts are not mere reactions to man. But the primary expression of God's sovereignty in the Old Testament is the proclamation of his moral will by which he governs history. It is this and not destiny that sets the ultimate and insuperable limit on man's freedom. Man cannot overcome the moral imperative; he cannot succeed in his ambitions by doing evil. If he does well, God will save him from the evil of history. This is a summary statement of the theory of retribution, and it is an imperfect statement; all statements are. Behind the theory of retribution is a belief in the difference between good and evil, which is not as simple a belief as it sounds when it is put so simply. Man's decision is important and has lasting conse-quences, both for himself and for others—for many others, if he is a person of some responsibility. The Old Testament affirms that there is a good and that man can achieve it; it is the sovereign will of God that he should achieve it, and history is directed that he should achieve it. There are obvious difficulties to which many Old Testament writers did not attend; we have already noticed Job's criticism of the simplified theory of retribution. The prin-ciple does not answer the problem created by men whose wicked-ness frustrates the efforts of others to achieve good. Yet the Israelites preserved this belief even after a national history which would tend to discourage it. Perhaps there is a dim discernment of the truth that the wicked man does not succeed without the cooperation of the virtuous, who are not entirely innocent when he attacks them.

This leads us to another consideration. The great literature of the world survives and is esteemed far beyond the time and place of its composition because it rises above the human condition and affirms, however vaguely, that there are values beyond the human condition that man must cherish. Great and enduring world literature has never been merely material-minded, never merely secular, never merely hedonistic. Neither is it other-worldly, a flight from reality and responsibility. We have noticed that the Old Testament manifests joy in life; aware as it is of danger and of pain and of mortality, it relishes the sheer pleasure of breathing and of movement, of integration with nature and with one's fellowmen, of the joy of work and of play and of achievement. Its joys and pleasures are simple, but they are also universal and easily available. But joy in life is tempered by an awareness that this joy is lost if it is purchased at the price of moral integrity. One may say paradoxically that in the Old Testament life is not worth living unless one can renounce it. Mere survival is not the greatest thing that the human person can achieve, and when life turns to a living death it is not worth clinging to. The Old Testament is strangely silent on the afterlife, of which it never exhibits more than a dim idea; but it does affirm certain transtemporal values for which one must yield this great good of life. It does not recommend suicide with the Stoics, nor does it share that foolish ideal of honor that one finds among the Greeks from Homer onward, and in much of more modern literature. It presents the simple conviction that the dignity of the person can sometimes be saved only by accepting death.

These values have been set forth in the same way in which similar values could be set forth concerning any world classic. We have made no attempt to show that the Old Testament is superior or inferior to other classics in these respects, but simply that it has qualities that are universally esteemed in literature that endures. Possibly most students of the Bible, who encounter the Old Testament as a religious document, do not attend to these values or never have them called to their attention. This is unfortunate, for the universal values of the Old Testament take nothing away from the specifically religious values to which we turn next. In fact they ornament the religious values by putting them in a humane perspective, a thing which believers often fail to do.

II

CHRISTIAN VALUES

The universal values of the Old Testament treated above are proposed with no reference to religious belief. Religious values of the Old Testament are perceived only by those who believe that there are religious values. The Old Testament of Christians is simply the Bible of the Jews; and Christians themselves are historically divided into Churches, most of which have their own approach to the Old Testament. But all the Christian Churches have the problem in common of explaining the values that Christians find in the Old Testament, and this problem can be discussed with no particular confessional implications. It is not the office of the Christian scholar to set forth the religious values of the Bible in Judaism; this can be done and has been done by Jewish scholars, from whose work the Christian scholar has much to learn.

We have already remarked that the Christian values of the Old Testament have been a problem for Christians since apostolic times. The history of this problem is highly interesting, but this is not the place to set it forth. But those who notice the efforts and the failures of modern interpreters to deal with biblical values should remember in compassion that they continue a long line of efforts and failures. For the problem is still alive today. The renewal which the Church experienced before the Council was a complex phenomenon with complex causes; but certainly one would have to notice some uneasiness about theology and its relevance to Christian belief and life. This uneasiness led the faithful to seek in the Bible something which they did not feel theology was giving them. The pursuit of biblical studies in the Church had been marked by purely technical studies rather than by work addressed to the Church as a whole. Biblical scholars were not ready to meet these requests, which were sometimes unreasonable anyway. This contribution to the problem cannot hope to escape the uncertainty that has afflicted biblical studies; we can hope for no more than to raise a few questions.

The incarnation is an historical event; it can be located and dated. As an historical event it shares the contingency that characterizes all historical events, and this in spite of the fact that it is a unique intervention of God in history. When the Word becomes flesh, a man is born; this man is a member of a particular human community and of a particular generation of mankind by nativity. Much of what he is has already been determined by the place and time of his nativity. The Word could not become universal man; he is qualified by those adjectives which we use to distinguish one human group from another. Jesus was a Palestinian Jew of the 1st century of our era; he neither lacked nor sought to escape the determinations that this historical fact laid upon him. It follows that he cannot be known unless these determinations are known. We do not imply that he cannot be known at all; we do imply that he can be known better if he is known in his historical reality.

It has been said so many times that I have forgotten who first said it that there are only two types of religion: the historical religion and the mythological religion. The historical religions are Judaism, Christianity and Islam; all other religions are mythological. The historical religion rises from an historical event, or claims to rise from history; the mythological religion is founded on the mythological event. The mythological event is an "event" improperly so called; the mythological event symbolizes some enduring or recurring reality. The historical event occurs only once. But the covenant of ancient Israel and the incarnation of Christian belief surpass other historical events in that they create an enduring reality. The enduring reality in a way transcends time and space, the dimensions of history; yet it never is detached altogether from these dimensions. In the New Testament the apostles call for faith in the risen Jesus; they are quite clear that the risen and glorified Jesus is the same Jesus whom they knew in that order which we call historical. They call for belief in his passion and resurrection, events which occurred in the world of time and space. They call for belief that God has once entered history in a unique manner, and that once having entered he remains in it. He can be found by those who seek him just as really and as surely as Jesus of Nazareth could be found by those who sought him.

Christianity was presented by the apostolic Church as the fulfillment of Israel. One may allege that this is the result of the historical accident that Jesus and his disciples were Jews, and that Christianity soon took on the colors of the Gentile world in which it found its home. But the Judaism of Jesus and his apostles was not an historical accident any more than Napoleon's birth in French territory was an historical accident. There are no historical accidents, unless one wishes to say that every event is an historical accident. Man must enter history, and God must enter history. There is no inner necessity that the incarnation should have occurred when and where it did, as there is no inner necessity for any historical event. Had it occurred at another time and place, it would have had a different set of determinations, but it would not have been undetermined. As the incarnation happened, it was clear to the apostolic Church, as it was clear in the words of Jesus himself. Jesus was the Messiah of Israel. There is no other title that describes him as fully, and the New Testament titles such as "Lord" are expressions of Messiahship, as are our modern titles such as "Savior". The very word "Christ" is the English equivalent of the Hebrew word "Messiah". Christians often use the titles of Jesus with no very clear understanding of the historical base of these titles.

When we say that Messiah of Israel is the only title that describes Jesus, we do not mean that this title describes him com-

pletely; no title does that. Nor do we mean that the title belongs
to Jesus either in the popular sense of his time or in its pure Old
Testament sense. In fact, "Messiah" is not an Old Testament title;
it was a word used in Judaism to signify a complex of Old Testament beliefs and hopes. Jesus transformed the title and gave it
new dimensions. But it was a transformation, not an entirely new
creation. In addressing the community to which he belonged by
nativity, he used the language and the ideas that were current
in that group; he could scarcely have done anything else. He
asked for faith in something that they could recognize; otherwise
they could hardly have been at fault in withholding belief. He
spoke directly to them in terms of the traditions that he shared
with them. Can one approach him if one is an utter stranger to
those traditions?

The apostolic Church did not think so. When the Gospel was
proclaimed to the Gentiles, it was the Gospel of Jesus Messiah.
The Old Testament had been translated into Greek for Jewish
use two centuries earlier; but it was the Christian missionaries
who were responsible for introducing the Greek New Testament
to the Gentile world. It is difficult for us to imagine how strange,
even how exotic these books must have been to the Gentiles,
unless we remember how strange they are sometimes to us. But
the apostles knew that a Jesus who was not the Messiah of Israel
would not be an object of genuine faith. A Jesus who was not
the Messiah of Israel would not have been for them—to use a
modern term—the Jesus of history, just as he would not have
been the Christ of faith. To proclaim Jesus in these terms must
have been difficult at times; to abandon these terms would have
made the proclamation impossible.

There was no lack of savior figures to whom Jesus could have
been falsely assimilated. Even to Jews it was necessary to show
that the reign of God was not the restoration of the empire of
David, and that the Messiah of Israel was not a conquering hero.
The material for this instruction was drawn from the same Old
Testament that nourished the dreams of an Israelite empire over
the Gentiles. Jesus was the suffering Servant and the Son of Man,

and his reign a reign of righteousness and peace in an entirely different way from even the ideal political reign. There was the figure of the lawgiver—not only Moses in Israel, but Hammurabi in Mesopotamia and Solon in Athens and Numa Pompilius in the legends of Rome. But Jesus did not proclaim a code of law, even a perfect code. There was Augustus, the bringer of world peace and order; a Roman poet saw his destiny announced centuries before. Jesus was not the conquering lord who imposed a peace maintained by a monopoly of military force. The title "savior" was commonly given to Hellenistic kings and was appropriated by the emperors of Rome; these rulers posed as the benefactors of the poor and oppressed and sometimes were. They protected their peoples against foreign enemies and brigands at home. Jesus offered no such salvation. There was the healer god Asklepios, whose cult became remarkably popular just about the beginning of the Christian era. The cures attributed to Asklepios in the votive tablets that have survived are not inferior in number or in the marvelous to the cures of which we read in the gospels. Yet in spite of the Gospel cures, Jesus is not simply a healer—for which the Greek word was *soter*, "savior". There were the gods of mystery cults—Isis and Osiris, Dionysus, Cybele and Attis and others—who promised a mystic communion with the forces of life and offered a cult fellowship that had no counterpart elsewhere in the world. No one could mistake Jesus for the god of a mystery cult. There was not then, and there has not been since, any lack of political or social or economic or healing or military Messiahs. It would have been easy for the primitive Church to transform Jesus into some savior figure who would have been more easily understood. As the Messiah of Israel he could not be turned into another secular or religious savior.

The Messiah of Israel emerges from the entire history of Israel and from the entire Old Testament. This means much more than a few alleged "messianic" predictions which, even taken together, do not convey the idea of the Messiah of Israel. In modern times it has become common practice to designate this history as "the history of salvation". The term is not entirely felicitous, but it serves the purpose of distinguishing the history of Israel from all other histories. One does not need to read the entire Old Testament to learn that it is also "the history of judgment". The polarization of these terms in the Old Testament is the major paradox of the Old Testament; this paradox is not resolved until the two terms are synthesized in Jesus. It is not merely that God is both savior and judge, titles that belong also to Jesus; it is the mystery that God saves by judging and judges by saving. Jesus is the ultimate revelation of the reality of God as judge and savior. The New Testament term that brings the two poles together is father. The synthesis is probably not obvious, and we must make some effort to explain it.

It is not true that the term father was first applied to God in the New Testament; it is true that it received a new depth and richness of meaning. But the use of this title was not one of the more revolutionary features of the teaching of Jesus. The father whom he proclaimed could be recognized as the Lord Yahweh whom the ancestors of the Jews had worshipped and whose saving and judging acts were recorded and sung in their sacred books. These books were the history of the encounter of God with Israel. They sustain almost to monotony the theme of God's faithful love versus the faithless rebellion of Israel. From what was it that God wished to save Israel? Not from its enemies, not from poverty, not from the dangers created either by man or by nature. The sword, famine, pestilence and captivity are almost a refrain in the words of Jeremiah. The saving will of God is not directed to these things, but to the radical evil that exposes Israel to these things. God can protect faithless Israel from the evils of history only by being untrue to himself. Israel has the knowledge of God and a way of life and worship that is worthy of him. If Israel retains the revelation and preserves itself as the People of God, it is saved. If it does not believe and hope in Yahweh, it must experience his judgment; for Yahweh cannot tolerate evil. He is merciful and slow to punish, but he cannot betray his promises by saving those who refuse salvation.

Thus the judgments of God are saving acts; for they move

against the evil that threatens man's salvation. It is God's saving will that Israel should be preserved, for Israel is to make known his saving will to all men. But Israel cannot be preserved nor can it be a messenger of salvation if Israel itself is a bearer of the evil that prevents salvation. The antithesis between salvation and judgment taken too strictly is a false antithesis. The human being must choose which of the two he will do; God achieves both, for his saving acts have a scope that man's saving acts cannot reach. The same union of salvation and judgment is applicable to the individual person, although the focus of interest in the Old Testament books is rather the collective Israel than the individual Israelite.

We have noticed that this saving and judging God is the father whom Jesus proclaimed and whom the Jew could recognize. Jesus was never charged with proclaiming a different God. It is the nature of love that it can wish no evil to the object of love. When Jesus reveals the love of the father, he discloses the ultimate union of salvation and judgment, the acts which always move to the good of man. That man does not recognize the benevolence of judgment is obvious; he did not believe it in ancient Israel, and he does not believe it now. Therefore in calling men to God their father Jesus calls them to a faith and trust that are ultimately directed to an unseen reality, the confidence which is given to another because of the integrity and the competence of another and not because the other has proved himself trustworthy. He invites men to commit themselves to a person who is altogether dedicated to them, and who can be trusted even when his actions are not the actions that we would choose that he perform. The judgment of a father is not the judgment of a magistrate; it is not delivered in favor of law, but in favor of the person judged.

A study of the Old Testament background of almost every important religious word in the New Testament would disclose that these words, like salvation and judgment, were employed with a definite traditional meaning. The Christian transformation of these ideas presupposes and rises from the tradition. Jesus and the apostles used a religious language they did not create, and without this medium the revelation of Christianity could not have been uttered when and where it was uttered. The Christ event, mysterious in any language, is most accurately set forth in its original language. When New Testament themes are translated into other idioms with insufficient attention to their original form, they become subject to distortion. Modern theology, in its attempt to return to the biblical background and expression of the articles of faith, does the best thing it can do to reach a deeper understanding of what we believe and to make this belief more meaningful for life

III

LIMITS OF THE OLD TESTAMENT

A study of the limits of the Old Testament is based on the fact that the Old Testament is history: the history of a people's encounter with God and its response to the encounter. "Progressive revelation" does not mean simply that God lets himself be known to a certain degree, withholding fuller knowledge. The limits of revelation are not the limits of God but the limits of man. Israel's experience of God, we have said, occurs in history and is limited by the contingencies of history. Its response to God is the response of which this people is capable at this moment. Revelation may be likened to education, and the comparison is often made; but it does not signify that the teacher conceals knowledge from the student. The truth is always intelligible, but it is not always understood. Revelation should not be conceived as a dictation of facts, or of "truths" strung together like pearls. It is a lived experience.

Thus, propositions cannot be taken out of the Old Testament and presented as if they had an absolute value. They are always a part of the historic experience of Israel and must be understood as such. Israel is not always a model for the Christian any more than the child is always a model for the man. Where Israel's experience of God is conditioned by its culture, the experience must be translated into another pattern of thought for another culture. And Israel's experience of God is always conditioned by its culture. Some areas of Israelite culture were never touched by its experience of God; and the Christian will do well to recognize that some areas of his own culture have never been touched by the Christian revelation. To illustrate from some of the points to be discussed: it is not accurate to explain the polygamy of the Israelites by saying that God "tolerated" polygamy among the Israelites and forbids it among us, nor even to say that God did not reveal to them another and higher standard. This is to view revelation as a dictation of facts. The transformation of man which the experience of God operates goes as far ultimately as man wishes it to go; and when he chooses to retain some elements of his culture, as indeed he must choose, he may be placing a limit on his own transformation.

Let us notice first that revelation in the Old Testament is largely set in the form of law. Now it is apparent to us that to think of God as a lawgiver is a very imperfect way of thinking of him; nor was the deity conceived as a lawgiver in the religions of the ancient world. Yet Israelite law was rooted in revelation, and the Israelite conception of divine law was original. Law was an expression of the Israelite belief that God had revealed a specifically Israelite way of life, and that observance of the law guaranteed that life was lived according to his will. Under this belief were included a large number of particular laws that had nothing specifically Israelite or specifically religious about them. The appeal to law as a way of life is quite different from the appeal found in the prophets, who never appeal to the motivation of law. How far this one-sided view of God could go is seen in the legalism that is repudiated in the gospels. Law is an imperfect conception of the moral will of God, yet it is a dominant conception in much of the Old Testament. The New Testament does more than simply correct the defects of legalism; the New Testament revelation refuses the form of law and does not appeal to the motivation of law.

Many theologians of the past have written at length explaining the abolition of the ritual laws of the Old Testament; yet "abolition" is not the proper word, for these ritual laws were never "laws" in the sense intended. The Israelites believed, and quite correctly, that God should be worshipped in a fitting manner. When one compares Israelite ritual with some contemporary forms of worship, one can see how restrained Israelite ritual is. Yet, what the Israelites found a fitting manner is again not in all respects peculiarly Israelite. The rites were external social symbols of a community attitude. They could be practiced without any reality behind the symbolism. Even some of the prophets represent God as asking sarcastically whether he needs the Israelites to feed him when he is hungry, and Amos and Isaiah represent him as saying that he hates animal sacrifices. The Israelites were unable to produce a ritual system that was not suited to their culture, nor should they have been expected to. Nothing illustrates better the limits which culture imposes than Israelite ritual. In another culture it is simply impossible and must be replaced by more meaningful symbolic actions. But whatever symbolic actions are used, no culture can escape the danger of employing symbols that are out of harmony with interior sentiments. It is remarkable how worship is one human activity that tends to preserve archaic forms after they are no longer understood—that is, when they no longer have meaning. When this happens, the correct performance of the action is all that can be preserved. A fitting manner of worship is not assured merely by the exclusion of what is obviously unfitting.

One does not need to read much of the Old Testament to learn that the Christian ideal of love of one's enemies does not seem to be mentioned, and that a very common type of hatred is often expressed. More than this, God himself is often identified with the Israelites' hatred of their enemies. This has been an acute problem for Christian interpreters since the early Church, and the antithesis between Old and New Testament here is so apparent that no solutions have been satisfactory. The holy war, with its total annihilation of enemies and the imprecations uttered in several of the psalms together with the threats against foreign peoples put in the mouth of God, cannot be combined with Christian love. Yet in the sermon on the mount this is one of the points in which "you have heard it said" is flatly opposed to "I tell you". Vague fears that the ideas of revelation and inspiration may be imperiled have kept Christians from taking Jesus at his word. Perhaps in no other area have Christians been so ready to take the Old Testament as an absolute as here. What God permitted once, he will permit again, when the conditions are repeated; and it is surprising how often Christians have found that the conditions are repeated.

No limit of the Old Testament seems to illustrate so well the principles stated above, that the experience of God transforms men as far as they wish to be transformed, and that adherence to a culture itself places limits on the transformation. For the Old Testament itself moves in the direction of the love of enemies. Together with such things as the holy war and imprecations there stand visions of a future in which all nations will be united under the reign of God, and expressions of desire that even traditional enemies may repent of their sins and believe in the one true God who saves. This is not a matter of "progressive revelation". Some of the passages that move toward the love of enemies are earlier than other passages that express hatred. Narrow nationalism appears both early and late in the Old Testament. This is not surprising; it was and is a common cultural feature in which the demonic in man is manifested. Christianity has not expelled this demon, and there is no reason to place it under divine patronage. Surely we should have no difficulty here in understanding that culture conditions the experience of God, and that we choose to retain features of the culture.

We have already mentioned the Old Testament morality of marriage. It may as well be said at once that the Old Testament in its laws and practices reflects the depressed position of woman in the ancient world; only the social depression of woman permits the absolute power of the man, polygamy, and the double standard of morality. Israelite culture was transformed in this respect hardly at all by the Israelite experience of God. What was needed here was not the revelation of new laws but a revolution in the attitude of society toward woman; and this in turn meant a revolution in the attitude of society toward the human person. The same need is seen in the Old Testament treatment of slavery. "The emancipation of woman" was not the key to the problem; woman was emancipated in the Roman world, but the process could not be called wholesome. Yet when Jesus announced the ideal of monogamy, he quoted the Old Testament; and the passage that he quoted says more than monogamy. It states the full human dignity of woman. Israel was not ready for the cultural revolution which this principle demands.

From these and other considerations that could be adduced, it is evident that the human condition in the concrete imposes limits on the effects of man's experience of God. Cultural limitations are in one way beyond the reach of the individual person; and where is one to lay responsibility for a community decision that is never institutionally formed? The analogy of the child is valid to a degree, as long as we remember that we are not dealing with children. Ultimately the limitations come from a free decision. If one attempts to give form to the unformed, one might say that the free decision is a decision not to accept God totally, but to accept him within the terms of the culture. It is not assumed that the experience of God will demand a cultural revolution if he is to be accepted totally; yet this may be just what is demanded.

If the limits of the Old Testament are so conceived, then the Christian may ask himself about the limits of the Christian revelation; for these limits also are not the limits of God but the limits of man. He will ask himself how the human condition of the Christian has placed limits on the fullness of Jesus Christ living in the Church, and to what degree the Christian community, or rather the separate secular communities from which the Church is assembled, have insisted on retaining their cultural forms. The Christian may even ask himself why there is no Christian community, and he will probably answer: because Christians do not want it. He may think that Christians have not yet accepted the revolution in the status of the human person that we associate with the Christ event, and that we still define the person in terms of purely secular values. The conclusion may be that Christians have not accepted God totally because they have not accepted man totally; and they cannot say that their sacred books have not revealed this to them.

IV

THEOLOGICAL VALUES

The distinction between "Christian" values as they have been presented above and "theological" values is not as precise as one would wish. Yet there is certainly a distinction between Christian belief, which is possessed by every member of the Church, and theology, which is a learned discipline in which only a few are educated. But theology presupposes Christian belief, and at the same time it nourishes the Christian belief by which it is strengthened. Furthermore, the educated Catholic in modern times is far better acquainted with theology than his ancestors generally were, and he desires that his faith be theologically nourished. Hence there is some overlapping between the two areas of discussion; we shall attempt to keep the two distinct as far as possible, but it is not possible to separate them entirely.

Theology as it has been developed in the Church can be called a philosophical interpretation of belief. By the use of philosophical categories and philosophical methods the theologian seeks a broader and deeper understanding of what the Church believes. He tries to relate the articles of belief to each other so that a synthetic view emerges. He reasons on the material so that new conclusions are perceived. He presents reasoned hypotheses with the purpose of answering questions which belief does not directly answer, or of explaining some aspect of the mysterious reality which is the object of belief. For several centuries the systematic study of theology has been dominated by the ideas of St. Thomas Aquinas and the school which bears his name. No other system

has appeared which promises—or threatens—to wrest the dominant position from Thomism. But it has been said more than
once that Thomism retains some features that suggest archaism
and a failure to speak to contemporary problems in contemporary language. Most of those who have expressed these doubts
have also expressed a hope that biblical theology will at least
help to save theology from archaism and from losing contact
with the contemporary world.

On what grounds should one hope that biblical theology, and
in particular, the theology of the Old Testament, might be a
vitalizing force in theology? We may first suggest the element
mentioned several times in the preceding pages: the fact that
the Old Testament presents the acts of God in history. There
is no system of ideas in the Bible; there is a sequence of events.
These events are recognized in the Bible as the unexpected, the
paradoxical events that foil human calculation and surpass human planning. They are instances of what St. Paul called the
folly of God. As such they might appear to stand in complete
antithesis to the reasoning of philosophy; this they do not, but
they are not readily subject to philosophical analysis, nor do they
fit readily into philosophical categories. The Bible is insistent
that the acts of God are unique.

In theology the awareness of mystery has always exercised
some restraint on the philosopher's instinct to rationalize. But this
mystery is revealed in history, and it is precisely in historical
consciousness that philosophy is weak. Philosophers from Soc-
rates to the present time have searched for a world of timeless
truth which rises above the contingent and the particular; this
timeless truth is indeed in some philosophical schools the substance of which the contingent and the particular are only the
shadow. Christian philosophers have been quick to identify the
supreme truth with the God whom they worship. They have been
less quick to see the danger of converting the God whom they
worship into an object of thought, and of failing to consider him
as active in history. Theology can become a system of knowledge
"about" God which, on examination, may turn out to be a knowl-

edge of what men have thought about God. Knowledge becomes more important than response and action, and this is not to deny the importance of knowledge; it is to deny that it is all-important. It is even less important when it is knowledge that fails to reach the object of its search and lapses into a study of the searching mind. The timeless truth is the abstract and the general truth, which is in fact the truth of no existing reality.

The meeting of God and man in the Bible is an encounter of living persons, and man responds to a person, not to an idea. He is called not to assent, but to surrender: to admit the other person into his life as a dominant force. He is called to become something other than what he is, to undergo a personal revolution. He does not know how far this revolution will carry him, and this is the heart of the mystery; he does not know how far he must rise to meet the level of God, but he knows that this is the height toward which he is urged. He knows that it is either all or nothing; he is not called to partial engagement that will leave him free to meet other engagements, other desires and ambitions. He knows that there is nothing in this life which he can be sure will escape the transformation that God works. He must be open to new and unsuspected possibilities, and it is not he who determines what they are.

The biblical encounter occurs in history, not in the timeless realm of the abstract and the general. God never encounters "man"; he encounters men, as individuals and in groups. He encounters Abraham, Moses, David, Amos, Isaiah. He encounters Israel at a determined date and place, at a concrete moment of history that will never be repeated. The response of men is equally concrete and definite; it is a response made in a particular situation, and it must reflect that situation. The response of one is not the response of another, for the demands of one situation are not those of another. Each one responds according to the needs and the possibilities that are his when he is called; and if his response does not reflect his personal situation, if the revolution does not occur in the real life in which he is engaged, it is not a genuine response. It is the response of the Athenians to

Paul's discourse: "We will listen to you about this some other time." The response is action, immediate and radical. The encounter demands a change, not the maintenance of the existing status. A change would not be demanded only in a situation that had no need of change. It is difficult to think of any human situation, past or present, of which this has been true.

The Old Testament "knowledge of God" is a misleading term, for we tend to think of knowledge as the knowledge of the philosopher. The proper word is not knowledge but experience; for the Old Testament relates Israel's experience of God. The terms it uses are comparable to one person's experience of another; these terms we call anthropomorphic, and we may think that the language of the Old Testament is moving poetry but not sound reasoning. No reader of the Bible can fail to notice that God seems much nearer and much more immediately active in Israel than he is now. Yet are we to think that Israel lived in a world governed by different laws from the laws of the world we know? If it did, then the Israelite experience cannot be meaningful for us. The acts of God were recognized in nature and in history, and the divine imperative was manifested in each of these acts. We may find the Israelite theology of salvation and judgment oversimplified, but it created a world they found rational. The removal of the active presence of God does not make the world more rational. God is as much an object of experience in our world as he was in the world of ancient Israel; he has not changed, nor has his attitude toward man changed. But man's awareness of him has changed.

The Old Testament affirms both the inevitability and the limits of the secular. Man encounters God in this world and in the activities of this world. He cannot find God by fleeing the world, although this recommendation has been made by a number of Christian authorities on the spiritual life. The saying of Thomas a Kempis, "Whenever I go among men, I return less a man", does not fit too well with the concern that God has for men in the Old Testament, and that men ought to have for each other. Israel did not have to wait for the Gospel teaching that men are judged by their dealings with other men; this it knew already. The teaching of Jesus on the love of one's neighbor is the hinge of the Christian revolution, but we have noticed that he spoke in a community in which this teaching was not entirely novel. The secular will pass, but it is in and through the secular that man will fulfill the imperative of God. He cannot disclaim responsibility for his part in the world.

We know that the Old Testament is a record of growth—not so much growth in revelation or in "doctrine", but growth in man's knowledge of God. The principle of growth should not be forgotten in theology; at least we should not think that Christian belief or theology has leveled off on a kind of plateau where there is nothing but horizontal movement. One need not introduce biblical considerations here; some knowledge of some of the remarkably primitive beliefs and practices within the Christian community is enough to show us that we are still growing. It was within the holy Catholic and apostolic Church that the Crusades were preached and witches were burned. Quite possibly the 13th century will find our Christianity as primitive in many ways as we find the Christianity of the 10th century. We too have the limitations of our culture; like our predecessors, we do not recognize them. But unless someone recognizes them, they will remain; for we compel the Gospel to come to terms with the culture.

The Old Testament can be studied as a record of Israelite failures, and studied from this angle it is quite interesting. There was really no Israelite institution that endured. The covenant of the tribes, the law of the covenant, the monarchy, even prophecy—all perished in the calamities of Israelite history. The few institutions that were restored after the exile kept Israel in existence as a cult group with a system of animal sacrifices and a religious law. But this group was without political self-determination and shows little of the creative force that appears in early Israel. It was a group that conserved, not a group that created, and in many historical crises nothing but such a group can survive.

No other people, ancient or modern, has written such a candid and critical record of its own failures. Law, sacrifice and king-ship are all the objects of critical narratives and critical prophe-cies that spare the faults neither of the system nor of the men involved in the system. Ultimately even prophecy itself ceased to be a significant voice in the Israelite community; the later prophets do not have the vigor of their predecessors, and there is no prophetic writing later than the 5th century. It is no won-der in this context that Jeremiah saw a future without institu-tions in which God would speak directly to each one as he spoke to Moses and would write his law on the heart and not on stone tablets. The failure of Israel to create enduring religious insti-tutions is a fact with some relevance; and the basis of Israelite criticism of Israelite institutions deserves more study than it has received. Historic Christianity has not been notably successful in the criticism of its own institutions. In both the historical writ-ings and the prophets, Israelite institutions failed because they were blocks in the approach to God rather than channels through which men could reach God. They were turned to other purposes than media of God's words and actions; they were employed for power or for gain, whether national or peculiar to the men who were responsible for the institutions. When the prophets pro-claimed judgment, they did not propose a reform of the insti-tutions; they simply predicted their downfall. Criticism could hardly become more radical.

What may these considerations suggest for theological method? No one knows better than the author that they seem vague and that they lead to no concrete suggestions. The study of systematic theology will not cease to be philosophical; but perhaps a shift of emphasis is possible. There seems to be no doubt that theology must become more strongly historical and more strongly biblical. Revelation is not a "doctrine" nor can it be stated in a series of propositions, however structured and organized they may be. Revelation must be seen as man's experience of God, and this means that it must be studied first, as theology has always recog-nized, in the Bible. But the strange world of biblical thought and language early drove theologians to the more familiar world of philosophy; and the translation has been less than faithful to the original. The experience of God occurs in the world and in history, and its effects occur in the world and in history. Revelation includes the divine imperative, which can be veiled; our own examples of a rather primitive Christianity make this clear. The divine imperative as an abstract and general principle of obligation does not carry force, and it certainly opens up no new dimensions of life. Theology in its treatment of the divine imperative has been more like the scribes than it has been like the prophets. It has had no room for the mythological pattern, for imagery, for appeals to the senses and to the feelings. Theology may say that this is left to other agents in the Church; but why should theology be viewed so narrowly? Why should theology avoid what is in the Bible the very heart and soul of man's adventure with God, man's encounter with God in history and the world?

An historical theology will place man's insights into the divine reality in their proper historical context, and recognize that no man speaks a timeless language; for God has always spoken in man's language. It will recognize the cultural backgrounds of revelation, and it will understand that if revelation is to continue to live it must be placed in the contemporary cultural background. An historical theology will abandon its excessive preoccupation with preserving the formulae of the past and its fear of venturing a new statement addressed to the men of its own time. It will not fear to do what the prophets of Israel did, believing that the God who spoke his Word through the prophets still speaks to man. The theologian ought to regard himself as one of the spokesmen of the Word, and he should not be content with repeating what earlier spokesmen have said. For to be historical is to recognize that history has not stopped, that the engagement of man with God continues in the present world and must be met in this world, not in some distant past. An historical theology does not view God as an abstract essence, and it certainly does not view man as an abstract essence. Man is never known, but the study of what man has been and done is a help.

If theology is to be historical, it will also be critical; it will not shun this part of the prophetic office. It will be critical of itself, measuring its own growth against the movement of history and judging its responses. It will be critical of its methods, asking itself whether its methods profit from the growth of knowledge as they did in the days of Thomas Aquinas. It will be critical of its own world, and its criticism will rise from an honest understanding of that world and from human sympathy with the men who live in that world. Cheap invective against worldly iniquities has long been the stock in trade of theologians who neither knew the world very well nor cared very much how it went. Theology has not often enough been constructive in its criticism of the world. Ultimately its criticism must be an utterance of the Word of God to the men of its time; and the Word of God is a Word of salvation and of judgment.

A critical theology will also exercise its criticism where no other agent is so well prepared to exercise it, and that is in criticism of the institutions of the Church. Recognizing that growth is a part of the experience of revelation, theology will know that the Church is always growing; theology should know where it can and ought to grow, and where its growth is retarded. Often theology has left this criticism to heretics and agnostics, whose criticism has been neither sympathetic nor constructive; men of these two classes have usually thought the best thing the Church can do is disappear, and that quickly. They rejoice when they think the Church speaks feebly and ineffectively, and they are alarmed when the Church engages in self-criticism. Theology has more often defended the institutions of the Church even when they were indefensible than it has attempted the kind of criticism of which it is capable. It has not always been so, and we believe that it will not always be so.

This attempt to present some theological values of the Old Testament is not intended as a contribution to method; the development of theological method is too large a task to be even sketched here. They are rather suggestions of a spirit and an atmosphere, a plea that theology can do much more than it is doing. It does not exist in the Church to be the night watchman of doctrine. It has its own peculiar responsibility of leadership which no one else can assume. Christian leadership can be learned nowhere more easily and quickly than in the Bible; and this is not to deny that the Church has known a number of leaders whose biblical grounding was not very deep. But whatever leadership they exhibited was an ultimate reflection of the Bible, which came to them through the Church which preserves and reads the Bible. Theology will learn from the Bible the power of the Word of God, of which theology believes it has a peculiar custody; from the Bible it will also be encouraged to release this power.

François Dreyfus, O.P./*Etiolles, France*

The Existential Value
of the Old Testament

I

THE PROBLEM STATED

We must first define the meaning of this title. The adjective
"existential" has been so overworked that its content has become
very vague and its outlines are badly defined. What I mean to
indicate by this title is that the value of the Old Testament for
a man of 1967 does not lie primarily in what it teaches about
God, about man, his destiny or his history, but in how it expresses
an experience of everpresent value, that of a meeting of God
with man, or rather with men. This is clearly expressed in the
conciliar *Constitution on Divine Revelation* (n. 14): "(God)
so manifested himself (to this people) through words and deeds
as the one true and living God, that Israel came to know by experience the ways of God with men . . ." This conciliar statement is in fact something rather new; it would be hard to find
any precedents to it in the declarations of the magisterium during the last hundred years.

But from another point of view, if we think about it, such a
statement seems appallingly banal. To those philosophers who
have reflected on historical knowledge, in the steps of Ranke,
Heidegger and Bultmann, knowledge of the past is existential or
it is nothing. I cannot understand a document of the past unless
it brings me some sort of response to my questionings on the

meaning of my existence. But equally, at the heart of the most classical Catholic doctrine, from St. Thomas to the First Vatican Council, it has always been clearly affirmed that God has revealed himself to man in order to save him, not in order to satisfy a legitimate desire for knowledge or to provide material for a theology. God, St. Thomas says, could have revealed to man other aspects of the mystery of his being, but he has revealed only what could serve man, to guide and enlighten him on his way to salvation. If then, as our faith asserts, the eternal life proclaimed in Scripture is man's genuine life, that to which God calls him to make his way, the value of a scriptural text, whether in the Old Testament or in the New, for the man of today, as for the man of yesterday or of tomorrow, is measured by its aptness to guide the decisions by which that man will choose the true life offered him by God. From this we must conclude that in the modern perspective, as in the classical view, the existential value of the Old Testament is the same thing as its value for the Christian called by God to the life in Jesus Christ.

But we must at once go on to say that the Christian does not need to ask himself whether any particular part of the Old Testament has a value for himself. He knows that the answer is affirmative. He owes this certitude to his faith, and it is the critical certitude of a Church whose teaching on this point has been disputed, but which has always replied with the same firmness, whether against Marcion or against the Albigensians or, more recently, in *Mit Brennender Sorge,* against the Nazis. It is not, of course, a question of just any verse taken in isolation, as if it were essential to discover its vital importance for the Christian of our day. But that isolated verse is part of a whole which requires all its elements to be of value to the man of today, or rather to the men of today. For our faith does not say that just any text is of value for just any man of 1967 in any concrete situation whatever. If the text is to speak to the man of our day there must be a certain resemblance between his situation and that of the hearers addressed by the biblical author.

This certitude of faith therefore invites us to discover the existential significance that any part of the Old Testament can and must have for modern man, in the conviction that such significance exists. If we do not find it, it is perhaps because we men of 1967 suffer from a certain *forgetfulness of the question* (rather in Heidegger's sense of the expression) to which the text is the answer, and the role of that text is perhaps to be a stimulus, to reawaken the question in ourselves.

We can now see what the task of the Christian exegete is. He knows from his faith that the Old Testament, not only in its totality, but also in each of the great units of which it is composed, has an existential value for the contemporary People of God. His task is to reveal that value. How is this to be done?

For certain elements of the Old Testament, the task is simple. It is easy to bring out the existential value of Job, of Ecclesiastes, and of many passages in the prophets, the psalms and the sapiential books. This is because Job and Ecclesiastes are *questions* raised by the man who asks himself about evil and the precarious nature of human affairs. On this level of questioning, the cultural gap between us and the biblical authors is bridged at once; these questionings, these problems, touch man in his deepest being, his fundamental anxiety, his agony of discontent. Here we find a constant, a structure. To use the language familiarized by Heidegger and Bultmann, we should say that we are on the level of the existential. It is the same with the many passages in the prophets, the psalms, etc., which challenge man by reproaching him with his self-sufficiency, his pride, his rejection of the elementary moral values, his infidelity to the God of the Covenant. Here again, the believer feels himself directly addressed, for he knows that his sinful heart is full of the same transgressions. All this is generally admitted and raises no question. It is not the same with the legislative and historical parts of the Old Testament, the existential significance of which is far from obvious to the modern man. To attempt a reply to this question, let us begin by asking ourselves how the Old Testament authors themselves solved the problem, for it was already a problem to them.

II

THE PAST MADE PRESENT IN THE OLD TESTAMENT
THE MEETING OF GOD AND MAN

The authors who collected the traditions relating to the history of Israel and gave them the definitive form under which we know them, wrote at a period already remote from the events they recorded. The problem of the meaning of these events to the sacred author was already present. It was all the more present, in that the historical concern, in the ordinary sense of the word, did not exist for him. His sole aim was to arouse in the hearer a decision of faith, of faithfulness to the Covenant concluded between God and Israel. In other words, the inspired author wanted to arouse in his hearer an "existential" reception, inviting him to be converted and to pledge himself to the Covenant, not an "historical" reception by which he merely accumulated information on his people's past. And as part of this plan, the author did not hesitate to present a version of past events that was very "present-making", neglecting those elements that were not likely to incite the contemporary hearer to a decision, but rather developing and elaborating, in relation to present situations, those elements that could provoke the believer to a vital engagement. I should like to clarify this by studying some particular aspects of the historical narratives.

1. *The Kerygmatic Structure of the Historical Books*

The studies of C. H. Dodd have made us familiar with the kerygma of the primitive Church; it consists of the two elements: *event* and *commitment*. The event is, for example: "Jesus lived, he died, he has risen, he sends his Spirit." The commitment follows: "Be converted, believe, be baptized." This basic structure, as we know, is found in all the New Testament writings. But this kerygmatic structure is equally found in the Old Testament writings; it is the structure of the Word of God itself. As the typical example, let us take the first commandment of the Decalogue (Ex. 20, 2–3): "I am Yahweh your God who brought you out of the land of Egypt, out of the house of slavery. You shall have no gods except me." The event of the coming out from Egypt, the liberating act of God, must immediately prompt Israel's commitment: "no gods except me". And this coming out from Egypt is treated not as a past event but as an everpresent reality, made present by the celebration of the Passover. The existing Jewish rite of the Passover meal contains, as we know, the following command, taken from the oldest traditions of the Mishna (Pes. 10, 5): "In every generation, it is the duty of every man to consider himself as having personally come out from Egypt." This command of the Mishna undoubtedly corresponds to the deepest beliefs of the editors of the Pentateuch, who were convinced that the People, in its successive generations, was a unity identical throughout. The actual People addressed by the sacred writers of the Old Testament *is* the People come out of Egypt. This shows us why the Pentateuch, in its final version, places all its legislative section during the sojourn at Sinai; this legislation is the commitment demanded of the Israel of today, identical with the Israel of yesterday and tomorrow, a commitment that is the response of man to the liberating act of God, making Israel his people.

2. *Deuteronomy and Its School*

In the historical books that follow the Pentateuch (Samuel, Kings, Chronicles), the two elements: event and commitment, are found again, but in a different manner. The kerygmatic aspect of the commitment is represented by the theological setting into which the stories are inserted, and which points out, for contemporary hearers, the present significance of the events described. In this respect, these books complete and explain the book of Deuteronomy, which is the clearest example of a "reactualization" of the events of the past in the light of the present situation. Apart from the concluding additions, the whole of Deuteronomy is in fact presented as an exhortation by Moses to the people on the eve of its entry into the Holy Land. The long legislative section itself (chapters 12 to 26) is presented as a call to the application of that exhortation. But the real audience of the book's author is obviously the People of God on the eve of the Babylonian exile. Yet there is no tension, no inconsistency, in this view of things. To the Deuteronomist, the people of the desert and the people of the 7th century are truly the same people, to whom the same word is addressed. It is quite spontaneously, with no contrivance of any sort, that the author makes Moses say what the men of Judah, 700 years later, need to hear. As G. von Rad says so well: "Deuteronomy blots out seven centuries of disobedience and places Israel again in the desert, hearing the word of Moses. But we must remember that this Israel is no longer the ancient people who lived below Sinai; it lives in a quite different political and economic situation; it is a wicked people (9, 6; 31, 27), and yet, as of old, salvation is promised for the present: 'Today you have become the people of Yahweh your God.' Nowhere else is this impassioned attempt to make the Sinaitic commandments present for the contemporary generation so clearly expressed as in the variations of that 'Today' with which the Deuteronomic batters the ears of his hearers. That 'Today' embraces in a single moment the time of Moses and that of Deuteronomy." [1]

3. Abraham's Sacrifice

This "making present" structure, event and commitment, can also be seen in the striking episodes of the historical books, even where it does not appear at first sight, wherever there is a meeting of God with man. We see it, for example, in the story of the sacrifice of Isaac (Gen. 22). G. von Rad has made it clear how the Sitz im Leben of this story is to be found in the problems facing Israel because of the divine demands that seemed to contradict the Promise. "With the order to sacrifice Isaac, God seems to annihilate his oft-repeated promise. In Isaac all was embodied, all that God had promised to perform for salvation. The story

---

[1] G. von Rad, Théologie de l'Ancien Testament I (Geneva, 1957), p. 204 (French translation from the 4th German edition, Theologie des alten Testamentes I (Munich, 1956).

of the sacrifice of Isaac goes far beyond all the other trials endured by Abraham and invades the realm of those extreme trials of faith, in which God himself seems to be the enemy of his own work for man, so utterly has he hidden himself; where he seems to leave to the man who has received his promise nothing but the narrow issue of total abandonment to God. Now it was just such experiences that Israel had passed through with Yahweh during its history, and it has registered the lesson they teach: Israel must know that in such situations, where God seems to contradict himself to an intolerable degree, it is in the presence of those trials in which God is tempering their faith. That is where the genuine meaning of the story lies, not in the traces of some tale of ritual redemption of a child marked down for sacrifice." [2] In this perspective, which is surely the right one, the story of the sacrifice of Isaac has a very definite existential bearing; it is a call to Israel to recognize its own history in this episode, and an appeal not to evade the demands of God, however scandalous they may appear in the eyes of men.

III

How Israel's Past Is Made Present for the "Today" of 1967

We can now see that if the Old Testament has an existential value for us, it can only be in line with and a continuation of that concern of the inspired writers of the Old Covenant. In order to discern it, we must bring the fundamental viewpoint of the Old Testament writers to light, in order to express it in terms of the cultural situation and the problems of the man of today. But here a vital problem arises: is not this existential value found in its perfect and final state in the New Testament, in the person, mystery and work of Christ? Do we need a candle when it is day?

One thing is certain, that for the Christian there is only one

[2] *Ibid.*, p. 155.

living, vital reading of the Old Testament, only one reading that
can answer the question of the meaning of his existence: that
which starts from Jesus Christ as its center, in relation to whom
every element of the Old Testament must be situated. Jesus
Christ is indeed the Word in fullness, addressed by God to man,
the Word in comparison with which all that preceded it are only
partial words. But that is the whole question: from the point of
view of their existential value for us Christians of today, have
these partial words lost their value, in presence of the total
Word which is Christ?

1. *The Answer of the New Testament Itself*

That answer is clear: far from making the existential value of
the Old Testament obsolete, the New Testament confirms and
accentuates it. The exhortations of Jesus (Mt. 22, 41–42; Lk. 4,
25–30, etc.), of Paul (1 Cor. 10, 1–13, etc.), and of the Epistle
to the Hebrews (11), are sufficiently clear by themselves, and
prove that in the eyes of the New Testament writers, the men
and events of the Old Testament have more existential value
than ever, as a call to imitation or, on the contrary, as conduct
to be shunned, or as a call to make the personal decision for
conversion. We have still to ask, obviously, which are the Old
Testament passages which, in the eyes of the New Testament
writers, continue to have vital value for the Christian. St. Paul
would seem to reply: all of them, on condition that we distinguish
their deeper meaning from their ephemeral expression and recognize that their value for the man of today will vary in intensity,
according to the subjects treated, the experiences recorded, the
legislation prescribed, the events related, and so on.

2. *The First Motif of This Answer: The Old Testament as Extension of the Potentialities of the New*

Jesus Christ is the Word of God in fullness, the Word addressed to men in order to save them, to let them approach the
true life in him. That Word recapitulates the former words and

nothing can be added to it. But from another point of view, that Word is restricted. In Jesus, God assumed a real humanity, which was therefore restricted in its roots and its concrete expressions. He could not assume all human situations. It was the same with the other characters of the New Testament. Again, the New Testament revelation took place in a very short period of time, dominated by the earnest expectation of an imminent Parousia. The aspects of the People of God involved in a long period of existence could not, therefore, be fully evaluated. Considerations of this kind enable us to understand how some episode of the Old Testament can show us, in an existentially clearer way, some aspect of the mystery of Christ, which otherwise we might not have realized to have claims on our obedience. Let me take some examples.

Faith. The New Testament writers, who so insistently emphasize the importance of faith for salvation, do not speak of Christ's faith.[3] Here, no doubt, they show their perception of a unique relation between Jesus and his Father, which is not adequately expressed by the word "faith", although, on the other hand, the attitude of Jesus sums up and brings to perfection most of the components of the attitude of faith. The indisputable fact remains that the New Testament writers, instead of presenting Jesus to their hearers as the model of faith, preferred to present the great figures of the Old Testament: Abraham, father of the faithful (Rom. 4, 11–12), Moses (Heb. 11, 24–30), etc. The fact is simply that the fullness (of faith) which is in Christ is shown more clearly, more imperatively with its demands for imitation, in the examples of the men of faith of the Old Covenant.

The temporal implications of the Christian salvation. For reasons that are well-known, Jesus refused to sanction the movements for political liberation that abounded in the Palestine of his day. If we had only the New Testament to guide us, we

---

[3] Some authors have tried to find the expression "faith of Jesus Christ" in certain passages like Rom. 3, 28 and Gal. 3, 22, but most exegetes have not followed them.

should find it hard to escape the impression that the Christian faith preaches indifference or resignation toward the various forms of political oppression. But if we consider the whole of the development of the idea of salvation in the Bible, we shall observe, not a lack of interest in the temporal liberation of the oppressed, but a change in the center of gravity. Jesus places the accent on liberation from the slavery of sin, without which all temporal liberation is an illusion, and only changes the mode of oppression. The episodes of the Exodus and of the Maccabees, read in the light of Christ, prompt us to evaluate the demands for liberation comprised in the Christian message (Exodus), the lawfulness of struggle and war where human and religious values are flouted (Maccabees). The passionate hope of an imminent Parousia may have led St. Paul to leave this aspect in the shade (cf. 1 Cor. 7, 21–24), but the Old Testament is there to invite us to take very seriously a human history that goes on (even if we are already at the end of the ages, cf. Heb. 1, 2), and which is to culminate in a total liberation of man, in all the dimensions of his humanity.

3. *The Second Motif of That Answer: The Old Testament as Education*

This is the aspect particularly emphasized by the conciliar *Constitution on Divine Revelation* (n. 15): "These books, though they also contain some things which are incomplete and temporary, nevertheless show us true divine pedagogy." Here again we find a dimension of Scripture which appears in the Old Testament itself. The educational value of the events of Israel's history for the contemporary believer is often underlined by Deuteronomy (*e.g.*, 8, 1–6); Psalm 23 transposes the great themes of Exodus to describe God's living care for the individual believer, and the final chapters of the book of Wisdom explain, in a somewhat unsystematic way, the permanent educational value of the events of the coming out from Egypt.

These different elements give us justification from the Bible for an interpretation which sees in the events of salvation-history a divine education, reproduced, *mutatis mutandis,* in the life of every man. Gregory of Nyssa was not altogether wrong when he made the life of Moses into a treatise on the spiritual life. That is the permanent value of the spiritual senses of Scripture, once we have eliminated the arbitrary element of the symbolic senses. God does not change; his ways are always identical with themselves. Beyond all the differences due to diverse situations and the sovereign freedom of grace, there are constant factors in the meeting of God with man, in the ways which God calls him to take, individually or corporately, in order to meet him. In the life of every man there is reproduced the long divine preparation, disposing his people to receive the fullness of salvation in Christ. For inside every Christian is a member of the ancient People of God, guilty, like him, of his murmurings in the desert, his unfaithfulness, his idolatries. The divine education of the Old Testament will always have for him (at least under certain aspects) the value of a sign, pointing out the road to be followed to his meeting with Christ.

These reflections have left many problems, which I have not been able even to mention, still to be discussed: the existential value of the prayers of the psalms, especially the prayers of vengeance and self-satisfaction; the stories of our origins, the prophetic predictions, the apocalyptic passages. There is a whole field here, still little explored. My object here has been to establish certain general principles, which may enable these questions of detail to be tackled.

In conclusion I should like to stress the relevance of these problems to the modern interest in hermeneutics. We cannot understand a text of the past unless we are existentially concerned by it. Now, how are we to feel ourselves vitally concerned by some Old Testament text, how are we to discover the aspect of our life which that text challenges? The "hermeneutic circle" does not, of course, date from Heidegger. Long before, St. Augustine had dealt with it at length in his commentary on the words: "If you do not believe you will not understand", in the Septuagint version of Isaiah 7, 9. The fact remains that any progress in the study of the existential value of the Old Testament is subordinate to the development of philosophical research on hermeneutics, and on the nature of historical knowledge. Our faith in the inspiration of Scripture does not diminish the importance of that research, but only makes it all the more urgent.

Franco Festorazzi / *Como, Italy*

"WE ARE SAFE" (Jer. 7, 10)
The Faith of Both Testaments
as Salvific Experience

The exclamation of the inhabitants of Jerusalem, which Yahweh forcefully reproves through the mouth of the prophet Jeremiah, serves as an effective introduction to the theme of faith. The temple sermon (Jer. 7, 1–15) presupposes an antithetical attitude to the one required by God's gratuitous and loving call. It manifests a shift from the religious response of faith to a magical cult which includes the idea of a kind of dominion over God himself. Carried to its extreme consequences (cf. Gen. 3: the sin of our first parents), this conception destroys the very roots of salvation-history with its emphasis on the idea that "[men] are justified freely by [God's] grace . . . through faith" (Rom. 3, 24–25).

A biblical treatment of faith must lead to the discovery of the living God as an active and salvific Presence in history: for faith is a total commitment on man's part to this reality; consequently, this reality will always be considered present—even if it will be considered only as a reflex—for the deeper understanding of the value of faith.

The aim of this article is to describe the existential content of faith in the living experience of both Testaments with reference to salvation.

A synthesis of the nature and role of faith according to the Bible should be preceded by monographic studies on the individual books or authors which for the most part are lacking.[1] The overall study of these would then follow, combining the historico-theological exposition (how God has *historically* and progressively revealed such a concept: the tradition and "traditions" of faith on the part of the People of God enter in as the "theological" part which prepares the decisive draft and the new significance of the inspired text, in its turn subject to an enrichment derived from successive revelation) with the systematic construction resulting from the overall vision of the Bible (what are its *essential components,* eventually the *center* of radiation, eternally present in the mind of God). The last step must lead to the understanding of the relation between the theme studied and the whole of salvation-history.

Obviously, even while taking account of this methodological approach, we are obliged to limit its concrete application. We will therefore propose a few reflections which we believe to be more interesting for a richer and more modern understanding of this experience of faith as described by the Bible. We will also indicate the essential problems that are still open as well as some suggestions for further study.

I

THE MEANING OF FAITH IN BOTH TESTAMENTS

The study of vocabulary in its semantic evolution deducible from various historico-literal contexts certainly possesses a fundamental value in the inquiry. From such an analysis we can con-

---

[1] J. Duplacy with good reason indicts such a deficiency in relation to the New Testament: "D'où vient l'importance centrale de la foi dans le Nouveau Testament?" in *Sacra Pagina* II (Paris, 1959), p. 431. An essential and representative bibliography on this theme in the Bible, put together by F. Dreyfus, is found in N. Nicolas, *Connaissance de la foi* (Paris, 1963), pp. 207–14. Cf. also A. de Bovis, "Foi," in *Dict. Spirit.* XXXIII–XXXIV, pp. 545–46; Ph. Delhaye, "La Foi," in *Ami du Clergé* 75 (1965), pp. 721–29, 737–40; 76 (1966), pp. 121–27, 618–22, 633–36, 665–70, 724–30. Some of the studies are outdated; others are rather fragmentary and at times a bit superficial.

clude that "the notion of faith is basically identical in the Old and New Testaments: 'to believe' entails man's complete commitment to God who reveals and saves".[2] For, this conception of faith corresponds perfectly with the historical experience described in both Testaments.

1. The Experience of Faith in the Old Testament

(a) *Abraham, Father of Believers:* Abraham's attitude of faith possesses an exceptional interest: the whole of the succeeding revelation regards it as a typical experience; furthermore, the Bible presents him as the initial depositary of a new and specifically biblical revelation, enabling us to discover in his experience the origin of God's educative design and the starting point of progressive revelation.

It is difficult to conjecture about Abraham's religious attitude before his call (Judaism and succeeding Rabbinic legends have deformed his physiognomy). We must be content with an approximate idea of this which in some way persists even after the call, as seems to be suggested by a few indications taken from biblical accounts. In any case, the religious experience of the election provides a decisive turn in the patriarch's life.

The Bible delineates the physiognomy of Abraham (Gen. 11, 27—25, 11), gathering and interweaving ancient "traditions" which take on their definitive character only in recent times (J, Yahwistic; E, Elohistic: 10th–9th century; P, priestly: 5th century). These represent a theological interpretation of history, and their integration adds new richness and depth to the original meaning.[3]

---

[2] J. Alfaro, "Fides in terminologia biblica," in *Gregorianum* 42 (1961), p. 504. The article (pp. 462–505) offers a fine semantic analysis.

[3] Cf. a panorama of the problem in the articles of H. Cazelles, "Patriarches" and "Pentateuque" in *Dict. Bible Suppl.* VI pp. 81–156; VII, pp. 687–858. In the study of the religion of the patriarchs it is necessary to carefully avoid every anachronistic projection; for example, Abraham's experience of faith would retain all its significance even if it were necessary to think of a total commitment on his part to the one God who enters his history without demanding thereby a monotheistic belief equivalent to our categories. Naturally, only biblical exegesis could resolve the prob-

The key chapters in Abraham's life are Genesis 12 (vv. 1–4a: J), 15 (E–J), 17 (P), and 22 (E–J); distinguishing the traditions is not easy, yet it is not lacking in interest even under the theological aspect.

Genesis 12 is essential for the understanding of Abraham's attitude of faith: this text in effect describes it as man's unconditional and total commitment to the *Word* of God.[4] Yahweh manifests his active Presence to Abraham as Lord of history and as Savior: that is, the *Word* comprises revelation, promise and dominion. Abraham's response possesses corresponding characteristics: it is a conscious commitment to the active Presence of God who reveals himself (certain acceptance because God is unchanging), faithful introduction into the salvific plane (protection—trust and hope because God is faithful), and the total dedication of life (active religious experience—obedience of faith—because God is Lord). Genesis 12, 4a, which concludes the episode of the promises, indicates concrete commitment to the Word: "Abraham went away as the LORD *had commanded* him."

These same elements of Abraham's faith are found in the episodes of the covenant (Gen. 15 and 17) and the sacrifice of Isaac (Gen. 22): the divine covenant with Abraham (a projection of the Sinai covenant?) creates the climate, the spiritual atmosphere in which his experience of faith moves; in such a context the sacrifice of Isaac acquires its fullest value.[5]

---

lem; in case of an affirmative hypothesis the monotheism would be the fruit of a successive revelation.

[4] The mystery of the Word possesses a fundamental importance in salvation history; cf. P. Grelot, *Sens chrétien de l'Ancien Testament* (Tournai, 1962), p. 126; F. Festorazzi, *La Bibbia e il problema delle irigini* (Brescia, 1966), p. 54.

[5] This is beautifully noted by G. von Rad: "The story of the offering up of Isaac goes beyond all the previous trials of Abraham and pushes forward into the realm of faith's extremest experience where God himself rises up as the enemy of his own work with men and hides himself so deeply that for the recipient of the promise only the way of utter forsakenness by God seems to stand open. Such forsakenness Israel had to experience in her history with Jahweh, and the result of such experience is made articulate in this story: Israel is to realize that in situations where God seems most unbearably to contradict himself, it is a matter of his

Genesis 15, 6 constitutes a particularly effective summary of Abraham's attitude: "Abram believed the LORD, who credited the act to him as justice." This passage indicates the patriarch's unconditional introduction into the plan of salvation—either as confident assurance in God's active Presence, or as complete renunciation of any human help. The divine covenant is the sole way of salvation and Abraham lives this reality in an all-embracing manner.[6]

(b) *The Faith of the People of God:* Israel transforms Abraham's individual attitude into a collective religious experience: "[Israel] believed in [the LORD] and in his servant Moses" (Ex. 14, 31; cf. 4, 31).

The theme of faith acquires a consecration and a special depth especially in prophetic literature and in the lives of the "poor of Yahweh".[7] Isaiah represents the most illustrative example because he combines the various recorded aspects in a rich synthesis, thus bringing the line begun by Abraham to its Old Testament apex.[8]

Isaiah is a typical representative of the "poor of Yahweh" (cf. note 7); however, as prophet he is especially the herald of the Word, constituted by revelation, promise and command. The response of faith requires a complete introduction into the salvific "mystery": it is a personal relation with the living God that entails the sure and trusting acceptance of the Word, the certainty of (messianic!) salvation, and absolute obedience along

---

testing her faith": *Old Testament Theology* I (Edinburgh & London, 1962), p. 174.

[6] A. Gelin nicely sums up this twofold component of Abraham's faith within the context of the covenant; cf. "La foi dans l'Ancien Testament," in *Lumière et Vie* 22 (1955), pp. 10–12. See also below, footnote 23.

[7] Cf. the bibliography given in footnote 1. The theme of the "poor of Yahweh" has particular interest in the problem of faith (cf. the bibliographical indications of A. George, "Pauvre," in *Dict. Bible Suppl.* VII, pp. 387–406, especially the splendid monograph of A. Gelin, *The Poor of Yahweh* (Collegeville, 1964): truly rich results would issue from the study of the Psalms (cf. for example, H. T. Kraus) and the book of Job (cf. the beautiful interpretation of S. Terrien).

[8] Cf. especially the monograph of S. Virgulin, *La "Fede" nella profezia di Isaia* (Milan, 1961).

the lines indicated in the theo-politics of the prophet.[9] The formal object of faith is therefore Yahweh as "the Holy One of Israel" (cf. note 17, below), an experience that also includes the salvific aspect: hence there is a spontaneous transition to the material object represented by the Messiah as Immanuel.

These Isaian characteristics are found in the various stages of his prophecy: In the preexilic part, for example, in the condemnation of Ahaz's negative attitude (Is. 7—12) or in the exaltation of Hezekiah's faith (Is. 28—33); in the exilic epoch, in the exhortations to faith of the Book of Consolation (cf. Is. 40, 27–31; 43, 10; 49, 23; 50, 10; 53, 1); in the postexilic period of reconstruction, in which the expressions of trust appear in contrast to idolatry and rebellion against Yahweh; finally, in the two Apocalypses of Isaiah (Is. 34—35; 24—27), in which the theme of faith takes on an eschatological dimension.[10]

2. *The Experience of Faith in the New Testament*

St. Paul and St. John can be called the "theologians" of faith for the New Testament: we will have occasion below to refer to the rich doctrine of the latter, limiting ourselves here to an express consideration of the former's thought.[11]

Since we agree with J. Duplacy that a complete study of St. Paul's doctrine and one which is in true perspective requires a chronological and structured investigation of his writings or those which are in some way attributed to him,[12] we will ex-

[9] "To enter into communion with God is to enter into a movement, to participate in a history which is of God. Participation by man in God's plan is, first of all, faith; and it is not by chance that Isaiah, who is the prophet of God's plan, is also the prophet of faith": E. Jacob, *Theology of the Old Testament* (New York, 1958), p. 174.

[10] It is not always easy to distinguish faith from hope; cf. *Lumière et Vie* 41 (1959), and above all the study of J. van der Ploeg and W. Grossouw (Old and New Testament) in *Revue Biblique* 61 (1964), pp. 481–507, 508–32.

[11] Cf. the bibliography given by R. Schnackenburg, *La Théologie du Nouveau Testament* (Brussels, 1961), pp. 70–73 (St. Paul) and pp. 86–87 (St. John); see also footnote 28 below.

[12] *Art. cit.*, in *Sacra Pagina* II, pp. 435–436. This is the ideal approach mentioned in our methodological premise. Cf. an example (a partial

amine only the most significant texts taken from the letters to the Romans (Galatians) and Hebrews.

The latter sets forth—besides a theoretical description of faith (11, 1)—a series of lived experiences in which appear the most famous figures of salvation-history, from Abel to the heroes of the Maccabean age (11, 4–40), all led by the *Word* of God (11, 3). The nature of faith, its relation to salvation and the unity of the divine plan are all effectively treated in this page, "one of the most eloquent and majestic passages of the Bible and all literature".[13]

Even more interesting by reason of the complexity and richness of the aspects treated is the letter to the Romans. One of the most important texts of the New Testament, it is representative of a greater "catholic" sensitivity: all men, without distinction of physiognomy or time (the universe itself is also included), are destined for salvation.[14] Precisely on account of this conception the salvific mystery as "history" is proposed with vigor and originality: the basic unity of both Testaments stands out in all its clarity. The literary framework itself seeks to translate this idea in a concrete manner: the dogmatic part, which speaks of God's salvific justice, cause of justification through Christ by means of faith (1, 17—3, 31), and of salvation, fruit of the divine love (5—8), indeed concludes the two sections with the living experience of Abraham (ch. 4) and the Hebrew people (9—11).

In this dynamic dialogue between God and man faith plays a central role. Romans 10—the chapter that examines the reason for Israel's infidelity—sets forth the essential lines of Paul's concept of faith: it is a total commitment to the Word (Christ crucified and risen, v. 9), based on security and trust in God

---

sketch) in M. E. Boismard, "La foi selon saint Paul," in *Lumière et Vie* 22 (1955), pp. 65–90.

[13] C. Spicq, *L'Epître aux Hébreux* II (Paris, 1953), p. 534. Cf. the excursus on faith, pp. 371–81, and the concluding section of this article.

[14] Excellent observations are found in S. Lyonnet's book, *La storia della salvezza nella lettera ai Romani* (Naples, 1966). Cf. also the following footnote.

(v. 11) which entails a way of life (obedience of faith, v. 16) and leads to salvation (v. 10). Similar qualities mark Abraham's faith, which St. Paul describes along the lines of Genesis, read in the original context (cf., for example, Rom. 4, 3 = Gen. 15, 1).

This conception of faith, amply explained in Rom. 3, 21ff., is continued in embryo form in the thematic sentence of the entire theological part of the letter: "The gospel . . . is the power of God unto salvation to everyone who believes" (1, 16), and is developed in the first section: "For in it the justice of God is revealed, from faith unto faith, as it is written, 'He who is just lives by faith' " (1, 17).[15]

3. *The Relation between the Two Experiences of Faith*

The analysis made leads us to the consideration of the essential moments of faith: the divine initiative as salvific call and man's response. This enables us to examine the relation of the faith of the Old and New Testaments,[16] avoiding an inaccurate perspective.

(*a*) *The Mystery of Salvation:* Salvation-history appears as a dynamic dialogue between God and man, tending to effect an intimate union: the encounter takes place in Jesus Christ, the God-Man, who is therefore its center.[17] Into this vision we must inject the theme of faith, either as content or as existential attitude. The first aspect concerns the divine initiative.

We return to the example of Abraham because it is most sig-

[15] S. Lyonnet has splendidly demonstrated the salvific significance of divine justice and the particular role of faith in justification and salvation; in this way he has effectively accentuated St. Paul's exact contextual interpretation of Gen. 15, 6 (context of gratuity) contrary to the reading of several passages of the Old Testament and Judaic literature (context of merit). The numerous studies are cited, for example, by T. Ballarini in *Introduzione alla Bibbia* I (Turin, 1966), pp. 441ff.

[16] Cf. the extreme case of the distinction between faith as "belief in" (Old Testament) and the New Testament faith as "belief that" in the thought of M. Buber (mentioned by J. Duplacy, *art. cit.*, in *Sacra Pagina* II, p. 431, footnote 1).

[17] A theological sketch of the Old Testament, composed of a theologico-historical analysis and a "systematic" exposition of God's plan, is found in F. Festorazzi, "Teologia della storia di salvezza," in *Il messagio della salvezza. Antico Testamento* II (Turin, 1966), pp. 619–759.

nificant. The description of his life demonstrates first of all the extraordinary intrusion of the living God who realizes the plan of salvation. It is difficult to give the precise physiognomy with which God appeared historically to Abraham. Neither is it easy to extract it from the tenor of the biblical account, under either its historical viewpoint or its theological interpretation. In short (we must avoid both a maximalism and a minimalism), the exact content of the salvific mystery appears problematical on this level of history and revelation. If we were to compare it with Isaiah, we should certainly have to speak of progress in the teaching of the prophet, even if it is not altogether easy to establish this entity with precision.

Nevertheless, we must resolutely affirm that revelation situates Abraham in the very heart of the salvific mystery: in other words, the motive and content of Old Testament faith (Abraham's example holds good for the entire Old Testament) is the mystery of salvation having as its base the living God, Lord of history and Savior of mankind.

Under this aspect the two Testaments are profoundly united and continue the same revelation of faith: it is therefore simply a question of a process of clarification and existential deepening which reaches its culmination in the manifestation of the living God in Christ and the Holy Spirit. The trinitarian revelation (understood not only as "idea" that is communicated but as "event" that is realized) is the supreme goal of the dynamic process of salvation-history. This highlights the identical character of the faith of both Testaments as well as the originality and freshness of the New with respect to the Old: the *progressive* manifestation of the living God of the Old Testament period, as it were, *explodes* in the Christian "Event" which transcends and illumines the expectation.

(b) *The Experience of Faith:* The concept just described becomes even clearer if it is considered under the aspect of man's response.

When we speak of the diversity of the faith of both Testaments from this point of view, we are accustomed to emphasize the intellectual side which would seem to be more (or exclusively) accentuated in the New Testament: for example, it would embrace individual events and ideas ("ordinary" and "extraordinary" episodes, truths, etc.). Yet it is debatable whether the faith of Israel does not also include an intellectual commitment to the Word;[18] but this does not seem the most precise manner of posing the problem.

Let us reflect on the experience of faith on the part of Abraham and the People of God: it is presented as a total commitment to the living God, Lord and Savior. This is how it is recorded by what is perhaps Israel's most ancient creed.[19] Now the life of Abraham and the chosen people is a patchwork of episodes which require the continual renewal of commitment to God: each is like a new "call" and constitutes a particular expression of faith. To reduce these events ("ordinary" or "extraordinary" interventions of God by means of episodes, words, commandments, etc.) to so many "abstract truths" ("intellectual formulas") would be to divest faith of its existential dimension.[20] This is something Israel never did; but neither did the New Testament: the "creeds" of St. Paul or St. John surely do not indicate a simple intellectual expression, but the penetration and

[18] The problem of the "intellectual" character of Old Testament faith is indicated in the bibliography given in footnote 1. With respect to Judaism, cf. J. Duplacy, "La foi dans le Judaisme," in *Lumière et Vie* 22 (1955), pp. 19–43.

[19] Cf. J. Schreiner, "The Development of the Israelite 'Credo'," in *Concilium* 20 (1967), pp. 29–40. See also the observations made in our article (cited in footnote 17), pp. 628, footnote 5, and 636.

[20] This is rightly affirmed by Grelot, in *Sens chrétien de l'Ancien Testament*, pp. 144ff. For faith—even viewed under its "intellectual" aspect—must not be reduced to a "sum total of interlocking theorems, reducible, so to speak, to their logical content. . . . It is necessary before all else to situate all these ideas in their existential perspective, apart from which they would lose all their meaning: that of *effective* dialogue between God and man, for which the divine Word represents the point of departure and faith constitutes the response. Such 'ideas' are immersed in the experience of this dialogue; they attain therein their entire real content" (p. 144). Cf. also A. Feuillet, "Abraham, notre père dans la foi," in *Vie Spir.* 253 (1950), p. 23. From this point of view it becomes evident that even in the Old Testament every single event is an object of faith (in opposition to Bultmann, *Theol. Worterb. z. N.T.* VI, pp. 216ff.).

commitment through the medium of events to the "intimate nature of Jesus, the secret of his being, the mysterious reality of
his person".[21] From this point of view, it is easy to understand
how even particular episodes and individual teachings can be the
object of the experience of faith: this is true for both the Old
and New Testaments.

II

THE RELATION BETWEEN FAITH AND SALVATION

The conclusion of the preceding paragraph emphasized the
substantial unity of the experience of faith of both Testaments;
must we then also affirm the equal salvific efficacy of both? Let
us here repeat—with greater emphasis because of its important
and delicate nature—that an accurate posing of the problem
must presuppose the impossibility of an integral reading of the
Old Testament except in the light of the New; on the other hand,
anachronistic evaluations must be carefully avoided.

1. The Salvific Value of Faith

St. Paul strongly affirms the efficacy of faith for justification:
"The [salvific] justice of God [is realized] through faith in Jesus
Christ" (Rom. 3, 22) is a phrase that sums up his thought very
well.

In the same context, as a biblical argument, we find the ex-

[21] I. de la Potterie, "La notion de Témoignage dans Saint Jean," in
Sacra Pagina II (Paris, 1959), p. 202. A less biblical (for example,
"hellenistic") notion of the concept of "truth" is possibly the cause of
the denounced ambiguity. For a fuller treatment of this theme, we refer
to the rich and exhaustive studies of the above-mentioned author, especially the doctoral dissertation at the Pontifical Biblical Institute in
Rome: *Aletheia. La notion johannique de vérité et ses antécédents his-
toriques* (Chapter III on John 14, 6 appeared separately) (Rome, 1966).
St. Paul is very close to St. John; cf. I. de la Potterie, "Jésus et la vérité
d'après Eph. 4, 21," in *Studiorum paulinorum Congressus internationalis
catholicus* II (Rome, 1963), pp. 45–47. Consequently, we must not speak
of a shift of emphasis between the Old and the New Testaments (trusting
faith; intellectual faith), but rather of a progress in revelation, which has
at its base an identical existential experience.

pression of Genesis 15, 6: "Abraham believed God and it was credited to him as justice" (Rom. 4, 4; Gal. 3, 6). The interpretation of the original text of Genesis is disputed.[22] We believe that the most probable meaning of this divine "justification" is an active introduction of Abraham into the salvific mystery worked by Yahweh. In other words, in response to Abraham's faith God has "acted toward him, so that he might be just". Cazelles admirably remarks that "this 'justice' of God conferred on man implies the whole economy of grace and salvation which St. Paul will develop".[23]

Obviously, it is a question only of a *revelation* in germ form (we can readily see the analogy with the theme of "life" in the Old Testament);[24] however, we believe that corresponding to this obscure stage under the cognitive aspect there lies a full reality on the objective side. Hence, St. Paul's transition from the salvific efficacy of the faith of the New Testament to that of the Old is not surprising; this transition is even clearer in the statements of the letter to the Galatians (3, 6–7)[25] and takes on

[22] Cf., for example, H. Cazelles, "Connexions et structure de Gen. XV," in *Revue Biblique* 69 (1962), pp. 321–49.

[23] *Art. cit.*, p. 334 and footnote 58. It is interesting to note the meaning of the two "traditions": the justice that God communicates to Abraham (Elohistic tradition) introduces him deeply into the messianic plan (theme of descendence of the Yahwistic tradition); cf. pp. 347ff. and footnote 129.

[24] Cf. the author's study *La Bibbia e il problema delle origini*, pp. 125–29; *art. cit.* (footnote 17), pp. 697, 730–37. Grelot (*op. cit.*, pp. 151–56) offers pertinent observations for a study of the theme of life with God in the Old Testament with regard to salvation. An investigation conducted especially on the Psalms and the sapiential books would yield very rich conclusions; it would also be just as interesting to see the components of this theme in relation to the historical, prophetic and sapiential literature.

[25] Cf. H. Schlier, *Lettera ai Galati* (translation of *Der Brief an die Galater*) (Brescia, 1966), pp. 132–37. In the same category it seems we must place the difficult text of Romans 3, 25–26: the entire Old Testament is ordered toward the realization of the promises of the divine covenant which is fully attained in Christ. Speaking of this period, Paul does not nearly intend to describe an historical moment in which sin is "tolerated" (not imputed) or only partially pardoned (a kind of inchoate justification), so much as he wishes to exalt the centrality and salvific efficacy of the work of Christ. That is why the "passing over" (CCD

a significance of salvific fullness which reaches to the resurrection in Rom. 4, 18–22.[26]

The same approach is followed by the letter to the Hebrews (ch. 11) in which theological reflection on history demonstrates the centrality of Christ's action: hence, it seems to us that the text points to a salvific situation with eschatological value.

2. The Salvific Centrality of Christ

The letter to the Hebrews, which "among the New Testament books is perhaps the closest" to St. John's Gospel,[27] has introduced the basic theme of Christ's presence into salvation-history.

Like St. Paul, St. John also reflects in his writings a historico-soteriological conception which contains and deepens the idea of "salvation as history" present throughout the Bible. Consequently, the two "theologians" of faith are also those who most acutely perceive the centrality of Christ in history.[28] For St.

---

translation of the Greek) of Romans 3, 26 (Old Testament) corresponds to the "remission" of Ephesians 1, 7 (New Testament; the context and terminology are significant), just as the "not reckoning" of 2 Corinthians 5, 19 is correlative to Romans 4, 8 (Ps. 32, 2; cf. also the "credited" justice of Abraham: Rom. 4, 3!). Cf. H. Schlier, *Lettera agli Efesini* (translation of *Der Brief an die Epheser*) (Brescia, 1965), pp. 63–64.

[26] Boismard, *art. cit.*, pp. 71–72. What has been said for the Christian reading of Genesis 15, 6 also holds good for that of Habakuk 2, 4 (Rom. 1, 17; Gal. 3, 11; Heb. 10, 38). P. Michalon nicely summarizes the relation between faith and justice, in the conclusion of his study concerning faith in the Old Testament: "Biblically, faith and justice seem to be truly 'the two faces of one and the same grace', because faith enables the whole man to enter into the mystery of God, and this mystery is a mystery of love that vivifies and saves" ("La foi, rencontre de Dieu et engagement envers Dieu, selon l'Ancien Testament," in *Nouv. Rev. Théol.* 75 [1953], p. 600).

[27] O. Cullmann, *Il mistero della redenzione nella storia* (translation of *Heil als Geschichte. Heilsgeschichtliche Existenz im Neuen Testament*) (Bologna, 1966), p. 365. Symptomatic of this is the importance that Abraham and his salvific experience of faith hold even for St. John: cf. John 8, 33ff., especially v. 57; cf. also 12, 41 in respect to 1, 14 and 17, 5.

[28] For St. John, cf. the work of F.-M. Braun, *Jean le théologien* (4 volumes have so far appeared: Paris, 1959; 1964; 1965; 1966: especially the last volume on the theology of St. John, specifically *Le mystère de Jésus-Christ*); for St. Paul, cf. A. Feuillet, *Le Christ Sagesse de Dieu* (Paris, 1966) (especially for the letters of the captivity).

John, for example, to recognize this and at the same time "to emphasize the relation linking the central eschatological revelation given in Jesus of Nazareth with *every* soteriological revelation granted by God necessarily implies faith in the preexistence of Jesus: the same Christ-Logos incarnated in Jesus of Nazareth must have been present (*efficaciously!*—our addition) from the beginning of salvation-history".[29]

This active presence of Christ in every period of history (even in creation which is its first phase) is a doctrine that is effectively and singularly resumed in patristic tradition.[30] The difficult problem consists in establishing its particular modality: we must admit that the most significant texts of St. Paul and St. John offer only a rough outline. They may however be sufficient to affirm an efficacy that goes beyond simple exemplarity, if we draw on the force with which they indicate the "meta-historical" value of Christ (as God-Man), alongside his "historical" dimension.[31]

Naturally, this does not allow a fusion or an identity of absolute value between the two Testaments: historically the division (expectation-realization) remains and ontologically a new condition of the People of God is created in the New Testament which becomes the historical prolongation of Christ (the Church).[32] We believe instead that we must affirm a more efficacious and definitive participation in the salvation worked by God in Christ even for the just of the Old Testament.

[29] Cullmann, *op. cit.,* pp. 386–87.

[30] Cf. a few indications in Grelot, *op. cit.,* pp. 156–61.

[31] To express ourselves in biblical terminology we intend to allude to the "pre-existence" of Christ the God-Man. Theology habitually considers the hypothesis of a *Verbum incarnandum* (with efficacious and exemplary presence), which becomes in time *Verbum incarnatum* (cf., for example, the reflections of J. Mouroux, *The Mystery of Time* [New York, 1964], Ch. VII); the historical glorification of Christ would render him present "meta-historically" in the whole of salvation history. A more accurate study on christology, especially in the thought of St. John and St. Paul, must, we believe, yield a more profound and complex vision of this presence of Christ.

[32] An example of this newness are the sacraments, which cannot be placed on the same level of Old Testament signs; cf. Grelot, *op. cit.,* p. 301, footnote 3.

III

CONCLUDING REFLECTIONS

The suggestions we have made seem sufficient to demonstrate the problems that are still open and susceptible of further study. In particular, we are referring to an accurate reexamination of the Old Testament in the light of the New: often our exegesis of it is still fragmentary and incomplete because it lacks this vision of the whole, and we run the risk of being minimalists.

On the other hand, we just as vigorously emphasize the importance of maintaining and noting the distinction between the various stages of biblical *revelation;* this does not necessarily entail a similar (at least essential) diversity, under the aspect of the ontological reality.

The centrality of Christ and its particular value is the theme that to a great extent awaits a new biblical study, accompanied by a patristico-theological investigation: a distinction (evidently not "an opposition") between "historical" and meta-historical Presence seems to us susceptible of particularly rich results. Not least of all, it might help to resolve with more coherence and in less simplistic form the complex and delicate problem of eschatology.[33]

[33] We refer especially to the earthly and ultra-earthly situation. Cf. a theological attempt at a new solution in von Balthasar, *Eschatologie, Fragen der Theologie heute* (Einsiedeln, 1960), pp. 403–22; the Italian translation of this work (*Escatologia, Giornale di teologia* [Brescia, 1967]) has a Preface by E. Ruffini, with pertinent reflections on this point.

Jacobus Vink, O.P./*Utrecht, Netherlands*

"In Yahweh Alone Is the Salvation of Israel" (Jer. 3, 23)

It appears trite to say that the experiences of salvation in the old Israel are attributed to Yahweh as their source. Yet, the statement is not without difficulties, as is evident from the fact that the various traditions gathered together in the Pentateuch are far from unanimous as to the moment when this salvation was for the first time recognized as coming from Yahweh (cf. Gen. 4, 36 and the accompanying note in the *Jerusalem Bible*). What in the present text of the Bible can be traced as growth and evolution has been organized within the framework of a genealogical pattern in the Pentateuch. The dividing line runs through the revelation on Mount Sinai. What does not completely fit into the Yahwist pattern is put on one side of this line—namely, with the patriarchs or, in the priestly code, with the covenant of Noah. In the present synthesis the event of Sinai constitutes the moment when Yahweh clearly reveals himself and when, therefore, one can clearly speak of "his people".

1. *Is Yahwism a Synthesis of Various Religious Experiences of Salvation?*

Today students of religion ask themselves whether the chronological order of the simplified picture given by the Bible should not be understood rather as a protracted parallel existence of religious interpretations of salvation experiences, including those that do not belong to the Yahwist type. And this leads to the question whether one can simply speak of Yahwism as such or whether this Yahwism is not rather a synthesis of various religious interpretations of existence which have enriched each other in mutual tensions and have become purified in the process. Since in the ancient East religious experience was determined from within by ethnic forms of existence, these types of religion must be divided first of all into sedentary and nomadic religions.

2. *Nomadic and Sedentary Types of Religion*

In the Bible this means that there is a tension between the Canaanite type of religion of sedentary peasants and the type practiced by small cattle owners, who formed the real backbone of the later Israel. It is less well known that, according to the data of the Bible, the religious experience of the nomads should be subdivided into two forms. V. Maag, continuing where Alt left off, showed in a recent study[1] that here we must recognize the importance of nomadic groups which moved from the region of the Middle Euphrates in the direction of Palestine. According to Alt[2], the patriarchal narratives of Genesis contain indications that these nomadic groups had a religion of their own which was marked by the worship of the "God of the forefathers". It is quite possible that the narrative of Abraham's vocation has preserved traces of a basic and profound religious experience of salvation. Maag quotes in support of this argument the so-called "transmigration" of a tribe of cattle nomads, the so-called Bactrians, shown in a documentary film. The starting point is a situation of extreme distress: the tribe or clan is forced by enemies or economic necessity to look for new pastures. The leader waits in seclusion and under great tension among his followers for some divine inspiration. This inspiration comes after a few days and with unwavering certainty the

[1] V. Maag, "Das Gottesverständnis des Alten Testaments," in *Nederlands Theol. Tijdschrift* 21 (1967), pp. 161–207.
[2] A. Alt, "Der Gott der Väter," in *Kleine Schriften zur Geschichte des Volkes Israel* I (Munich, 1959), pp. 1–78.

leader takes his people with tremendous effort across a high mountain range. After a journey with heavy losses in men and cattle the exhausted tribe finally arrives in a region of abundant pastures, and the divine promise comes true. There is every reason to believe that a crisis of similar proportions lay at the root of the biblical injunction given to Abraham to go to the land "which I shall show you". In the science of religion it is a constantly recurring fact that such drastic crises in existence often lead to a major religious breakthrough. The "ancestral divinity" type of religion as found in the stories of Abraham, Isaac and Jacob, and also rediscovered among the Nabataeans, is marked by the divinity accompanying the clan on its journeys. On the part of the people there is here a corresponding attitude of faith and trust, based on this fundamental saving experience of God as "he who leads men toward a new existence". The characteristics of the divinity are not so much awe-inspiring as trust-inspiring, a divinity with whom the people live on a footing of familiarity. There is no separate class of ministers for worship, and the sacrifice is less the offering of many animals as a gift than a communal meal with this divinity. In origin these first nomads are clearly distinct from the Sinaitic-Egyptian group of nomads whose saving experience was from the beginning linked up with Yahweh, their own God. Whether the name of this God was originally taken from the Midianites or not need not be discussed here. In contrast with the group mentioned above, these nomads saw their salvation far more as a process of being saved from *enemies*.

3. *The Synthesis of These Two Types*

It was once again a crisis which threatened their existence that brought both groups as well as their religious experiences together. Both groups tried to find a way into the no-man's-land of Palestine which lay open for them between the strong city-states of the Canaanites. The threat to their existence from these city-states made them link up in a *covenant*, elements of which we can still see in the text of Joshua 24 (for example,

vv. 2, 14 and 15), in spite of later revisions. According to Maag
the importance of the covenant, so essential an element in the
religion of Israel in all its later forms, dates from this time. The
saving experience of Yahweh's intervention at the exodus
spread, one would almost say, like a contagion. The group of
related clans and tribes, all claiming the tradition of this salvation as their own, grew constantly. All the saving experiences
of the "ancestral divinity" were absorbed in these Yahwist traditions. In the center of it all stood the epiphany of Yahweh
on Mount Sinai. The pilgrimages to the desert sanctuary became
so deeply engraved into the minds of these groups of nomads that
the description of the awe-inspiring God who showed himself
there as the destroyer of enemies in the wars of Yahweh remained central for all later generations. Yet a far greater crisis
loomed on the horizon of these tribes. The Philistines, a far
fiercer and more recent arrival in the coastlands of Palestine
than the city-states of the Canaanites, required a far stronger
alliance of the related tribes than before.

4. *The Religious Function of the Monarchy*

Only at this time did the *monarchy* appear in the history of
these tribes. In this they were "behind", compared with their
environment. This only possible way of meeting the Philistine
menace, first a failure under Saul, then successful under David,
meant that the ethnic and therefore also the religious type of
Canaan was absorbed by the tribes, who only then formed for
the first time what we know as "Israel". More recent studies
(cf. Herrmann and Maier[3]) have rejected the thesis, upheld by
Noth since 1930 and accepted by many, that Israel as the alliance of twelve tribes had already been achieved before the
monarchy in the time of the Judges, and that this alliance rested
on common links with one sanctuary (amphictyony). It is
rather the case that once again a threat to existence led to
political and strategic—and at the same time religious—creativ-

[3] S. Herrmann, "Das Werden Israels," in *Theol. Liter. Zeit.* 87 (1962),
pp. 561–74; J. Maier, *Das altisraelitische Ladeheiligtum* (Berlin, 1965).

ity, for these were always closely intertwined in the ancient East. All the traditions of Yahweh as warrior came to life in the general levy, the popular army, the gathering of which from such different tribes was already a stroke of genius of David. There Yahweh revealed himself as the Yahweh Sabaoth: the Yahweh of the two armies (the interpretation of the word as a dual form is J. Maier's and seems to me a brilliant explanation of 1 Kings 2, 5 and 2 Sam. 11, 11). According to Maier, it was also under David that the Ark became central as the safeguard of the people. After the conquest of Jerusalem the Canaanites become integrated into the Israelite State which now came into being, and the foundations could be laid for that ideology of kingship which was so important for the sedentary experience of religion. In contrast with the nomadic religious experience, the sedentary type is far more static and "cyclic", and far more concentrated on the forces inherent in vegetation. This static order, "statically" threatened by the powers of chaos, is dominated by the creator and highest God: El. A parallel situation existed in Babylon and in Canaanite Palestine: just as this highest God sends a lower god, Baal, to fight the chaos, so he places the king in the land to protect the community of his people from chaos. Around this king a class of ministers of worship grows, charged with what for the Israelites of nomadic traditions must have been a new and strange experience—namely, the offering of burnt offerings or holocausts. The whole burnt animal is offered to the divinity as a present. In the Canaanite cult-community, which was truly magic in mentality, this must have meant a strengthening of the divinity in his task of preserving the world. There are also wise men at this Egyptian-style court. All traditions are being rethought and as far as possible fused together.

5. The Dating of the Earliest Scriptural Traditions

Only now have we reached the point where we must put the date of *the earliest tradition of the written Pentateuch*, the Yahwist tradition, and we should keep this basic fact firmly in mind.

The whole process mentioned above, a process of encounter, enrichment, addition and purification of religious experiences, has then already taken place under the pressure of threats which beset those fragile and defenseless tribes and tribal groups. The systematized, chronological, and genealogical succession of the saving deeds of God, as we read of them now in the Bible, is certainly the reflection of saving experiences attributed in faith to Yahweh. But I hope that what has been said has made it clear that what has been described there does not immediately correspond to the experience of salvation but is for a large part a projecting back, on a magnifying scale, into primitive times.

6. *The Genesis of the Religious Experience of Salvation*

When in the Israel of the monarchy the great geographic barriers had been pulled down, which until then had allowed the three groups of tribes (North, Middle and South) to lead a relatively independent existence, and when the fatal threat of the Philistines had been met, it became inevitable that the achievement of unity, greatness and military success under David was projected back into the sacred origins of the primitive age. The original data—the grant of new pastures to cattle-owning nomads in extreme distress, the deliverance of nomads on the borders of Egypt and, finally, the yearly cycle of the soil's fertility—are preserved. Moreover, the synthesis of all the traditions is marked by the *exclusive* character of Yahwism: Yahweh tolerates no gods by his side. But beyond this, the unity which is in fact achieved only very laboriously, was projected back to the first beginnings: all the twelve tribes are taken safely through the sea along the wall of water which allowed their passage; the gradual infiltration of the country by rather weak nomadic tribes is surrounded with the halo of a miraculous lightning war (compare Judges 1 with Joshua 5—12). The Ark, symbol of David's successes, is described as already present in the desert. The stories of the patriarchs become pegs on which Israel hangs its own experience and the struggle of its faith. The revelation on Mount Sinai becomes the central point which gathers all the laws from every period in the existence of the people of Israel into a coherent unity. All the elements of unity and stability, security and safety, of the full-grown State of Israel are attributed to Yahweh in such a way that it looks as if they already existed in that holy age of Yahweh, the age of those primitive origins, when Yahweh began to mold Israel. It is not as if the early monarchy was seen as the end and final rest. The mutual tensions and interplay of the two most evident poles in this whole field of various forces—namely, the nomadic culture and the sedentary culture—continued for centuries. It was above all the task of the prophets to keep an eye on this interplay. The prophets saw the gravest temptations in those elements of the sedentary religious culture which might be interpreted as sanctions of the established power and of tangible and available security. Perhaps the clearest illustration of this may be found in Chapters 7 and 26 of Jeremiah which describe the false security which many found in the temple. Yet, this sedentary religious culture also made a positive contribution: *messianism* is unthinkable without the ideology of the monarchy, just as, on the other hand, the dynamism of this Israelite messianism, oriented toward the future, is unthinkable without that character of the promise for the future which was typical of the nomadic religious mentality, as Maag has pointed out.

7. *The View of Henry Renckens*

Does all that has been said conflict with what is usually said about it by believing authors? The reading of Henry Renckens' *The Religion of Israel* might lead to this conclusion.[4] "Thus Israel herself provides a radically superhuman interpretation of the strange phenomenon in which her origin and development were exempt from the normal laws of history, and, what is perhaps even more noteworthy, her religion did not fit into any of the normal patterns recognized by scholars of comparative religion. God took a hand in the growth and historical development of this nation. *He shaped Israel in a way which far transcended the*

[4] H. Renckens, *The Religion of Israel* (Sheed & Ward, 1967).

normal course of divine providence, and by so doing the creator of heaven and earth decreed the fate of all nations and bore in his hand the hearts of kings and rulers. . . . The Christian interpretation of the phenomenon of Israel is in complete accord with the Jewish interpretation, in acknowledging this divine factor. Israel is thus as much a mystery as the phenomenon of Christianity is a mystery, and Israel is furthermore directly implicated in this mystery. It is, however, a mystery which cannot be proved as such. It can only be substantiated when it is approached with faith, or better, when it is experienced as a living reality. It should, however, be noted at this point that it is not the author's intention to lose himself in needless argument with unshakably convinced rationalists, in a book aimed first and foremost at believers. *Having postulated, then, that this mystery is a fact of history,* it is advisable to express the factuality of the mystery in all its aspects. This expression is not so much directed toward convincing those who already believe, as attempting to ascertain the exact place which the mystery of Israel occupies in Christian faith, and the precise extent to which this mystery is, both in the case of the individual and in its application to the Christian community, life of the Christian life" (pp. 2–3).

This quotation, the italics in which are mine, prompts the vast question why there should be a conflict between the believing interpretation, the believer seeing it as mystery, the recognition of God's influence, on the one hand, and the fitting into the ordinary laws of history and the ordinary patterns of comparative religion on the other. Why must these two exclude each other? Is it necessary that the believing analysis should be a *causal* analysis? Is it necessary for the faithful to describe the objective mutual relations between events and mental processes in a way which is detached from the faithful's interpretation of their own existence? Although we may admit that neither the biblical authors nor many generations of Christians have made these distinctions, this does not relieve *us,* living in the 20th century and able to use sciences whose object is the study of what is objective and causal in texts, from the obligation to make these distinctions. Moreover, is it necessary that a scientific study of Israel's religion which aims *in principle* at a *full causal* explanation should exclude the use of biblical language ("mystery", "God's hand") when one speaks "in faith" (e.g., in the liturgy), even though one recognizes the legendary character of much of this language? On the answer to these questions will depend whether Renckens can discuss the matter (in a not necessarily laborious manner), not with "confirmed rationalists" but with believers who have, for themselves, already formulated an answer. In such a discussion the author would be first of all invited to explain what he means when he says that "the mystery is a fact of history". His partner in the dialogue would point out that he, too, lets the factual aspect speak for itself in every way and, above all, that he, too, seeks to find out what part Israel's mystery plays in his Christian creed and in what way it is for the Christians, individually and collectively, a living of one's own life. Perhaps we may leave this controversy alone and conclude this article with a few observations, prompted by this last question. In other words: What are the constant and varying elements in this saving experience of the faithful in the Old and the New Testaments? A full answer would require another article. Yet some answers are, as it were, implied in all that has been said above.

8. *The Experience of Religious Salvation in the Old and New Testaments*

It may perhaps be said that the religious experiences of salvation in the Old Testament have in common the qualities of being *collective* and *institutional*. Specific collective groups, as we have seen, were threatened in their existence. The image of God, which was operative every time in the religious interpretation of the salvation which followed the threat, was therefore always marked by the characteristics of the particular group. Yahweh was the shepherd, he who by the power of his Word and promise led the way to a new existence, still hidden in the future. Yahweh was the warrior who destroyed nations as the

Israelites advanced. Yahweh was the king who guaranteed the blessings of nature and checked the forces of chaos which threatened the Israelites via foreign nations. This king demanded his sacrifices, many animals from the herds that increased through his benevolence. There was also room for the individual as is evident from some passages in the psalms and appears, paradoxically enough, in texts which speak of doubt and bewilderment about God and of which there are a great number in the Bible. The function of the wise man, highly respected because of his connections with the court, allows for a certain degree of individuality, although here, too, it seems to occur mainly in the most skeptical among wise men, the preacher. The visions which call forth the various prophets manifest a strongly individual experience of God, although recent biblical studies have shown how much, for instance, Isaiah 6 is impregnated with stereotyped expressions belonging to cultic ministers at the court.

Would it be correct to say that in the New Testament the experience of God is described in terms that show rather the threatened existence of man as an *individual?* In this we think of the suffering of Christ himself as the Suffering Servant, as well as of the suffering mentioned in the parable of the Good Samaritan which speaks about interpersonal relations. It seems to me that the New Testament criticizes the Old Testament particularly where the Old Testament institutions threaten to become an obstacle which may cause us to overlook the needs of the human individual. Through Jesus God is brought closer to man, and this in the sense that in the new image of God many barriers are broken down that were still accepted in the Old Testament, such as nationalism, moral classes and degrees among men ("This man eats with publicans and sinners"), age, sex, ability and knowledge.

A very different question is whether this description of what is new in the New Testament is applicable to every book of this New Testament. In other words, the question is whether the distinction between books of the Old and the New Testaments is as watertight as is sometimes thought. It might be, for instance, that in Paul and Matthew certain strands of the Old Testament continue to operate even where they create a certain tension with the new elements brought about by Jesus. In spite of this criticism this Old Testament remains the Bible of Jesus and of us because we discover *within* these collective groups and institutions *human beings* whom we recognize as our brothers in their need of faith and with whom we want to praise God *together.*

Elpidius Pax, O.F.M. / *Jerusalem, Jordan*

Fulfilling the Commandment (Deut. 6, 25)

"And it will be righteousness for us, if we are
careful to do all this commandment . . ." (Deut. 6, 25)

Today's Christian will probably be surprised on first hearing
these words of Deuteronomy. They do seem to belong to an epoch
that has long since been superseded by the New Testament. We
recall Paul's opposition to the Judaism of his day, which believed
that exact observance of the law would guarantee salvation.
Moreover, law and gospel are frequently, even if mistakenly, set
up in opposition to one another. The freedom of God's children
seems to display itself in man's ability to freely develop all his
talents to the fullest and thus draw closer to God. As we see it, a
multiplicity of legal prescriptions represents a restriction on our
personality. Nowhere is the Christian's critical attitude toward
the Old Testament more evident than on the question of law.

I

THE BIBLICAL CONTEXT

Of course we cannot consider such a citation in isolation. We
must frame it within its original context. Here is the full context
in Deuteronomy:

When your son asks you in time to come: "What is the meaning of the testimonies and the statutes and the ordinances which the Lord our God has commanded you?" then you shall say to your son:

"We were Pharaoh's slaves in Egypt; and the Lord brought us out of Egypt with a mighty hand; and the Lord showed signs and wonders, great and grievous, against Egypt and against Pharaoh and all his household, before our eyes; and he brought us out from there, that he might bring us in and give us the land which he swore to give to our fathers. And the Lord commanded us to do all these statutes, to fear the Lord our God, for our good always, that he might preserve us alive, as at this day. And it will be righteousness for us, if we are careful to do all this commandment before the Lord our God, as he has commanded us." [1]

This context sheds a different light on our problem. We are dealing with a catechetical instruction, such as that which is found in the Jewish home liturgy to this very day. It is the younger generation, the son, who asks about the meaning of the law. This generation knows its people's history only from hearsay; to it many things may seem old-fashioned and out of date. Thus the text relates very much to our own religious situation. For not only are we further removed in time from this history, we actually live in a completely altered environment.

In answering the boy's question, his father does not tackle it at once. He first centers on the great salvific events—the liberation of Israel from Egypt and its deliverance into the promised land. God does these things because he is the giver of life. *Life* is the leitmotif of our citation. But life is to be preserved and

[1] Deut. 6, 20–25. Biblical citations are taken from the *Revised Standard Version*. See the following modern commentaries on the decalogue: G. von Rad, *Theologie des Alten Testamentes* I (Munich, 1957), pp. 192–230; J. J. Stamm, *Der Dekalog im Lichte der neueren Forschung*, Bern, [2]1961; J. J. Stamm, "Dreissig Jahre Dekalogforschung," *Theol. Rundschau* 27 (1961), pp. 189–231; H. Graf Reventlow, *Gebot und Predigt im Dekalog* (Gütersloh, 1962); J. Schreiner, *Die Zehn Gebote im Leben des Gottesvolkes* (Munich, 1966).

maintained in accordance with God's will; that is, the people must submit to his ordinances. If his people do this, they will be "righteous". This concept, as we shall see, is closely bound up with the notions of "life" and "salvation".

But how can commandments give life? That is the critical question to which we now turn our attention.

II

COMMANDMENT AND LIFE

When we talk here about statutes and commandments, we mean all the laws to be found in the book of the Covenant (Exod. 20, 22–23, 19), in the law of holiness (Lv. 17–26), and in Deuteronomy (Deut. 12–26). But these frequently represent time-conditioned clarifications and elaborations of the decalogue, so the relationship between law and life must be explained in terms of the decalogue itself.

The Sinai event—the handing down of the law—made an indelible impression on the memory of the Hebrew nation. God's appearance (theophany) in the midst of their wanderings in the desert took place under extraordinary circumstances; hence the precise details of what happened is unimportant. In this theophany the Israelite nation saw God breaking into the world of men. Thus the handing down of the law acquired a special character.

This theophany, however, is not an isolated happening. They characteristically take place at critical junctures in Israel's history—e.g., the call of Moses (Exod. 3), the establishment of the Covenant (Gen. 17), the pledge made to Abraham (Gen. 18), the guiding pillars of cloud and fire (Exod. 13, 21), the conquest of Palestine (Jos. 5, 13). As a matter of fact we find a theophany at the very start of creation; all nature—mankind in particular—owes its existence to the appearance of God and his spoken commands.[2]

One of Michelangelo's paintings in the Sistine Chapel superbly

[2] E. Pax, *Epiphaneia* (Munich, 1955), pp. 100–44.

captures the moment when Adam awakes to life through the unexpected touch of God's hand. One of Marc Chagall's glass paintings in the Synagogue at Jerusalem depicts the twelve tribes of
Israel; and the play of light and color seems to hint at the mysterious presence of God forming his people into a community. In
Chagall's representation of the tribe of Levi we see the crimson
and violet tablets of the decalogue, and we read these words:
"They shall teach Jacob thy ordinances, and Israel thy law"
(Deut. 33, 10). Then there is the chalice of salvation, overflowing
with fruits and flowers, and the delicate gold hue that represents
the sun and the divine light.[3] Chagall has captured the meaning
of our text superbly.

The law derives from the creative power of a loving God. Its
purpose is to foster man's full development within a community
that God has established for him. God's creative power is also
a redemptive power, saving his people from a world that opposes
him: "The Lord brought us out of Egypt" (Deut. 6, 21). If his
people observe his laws, they will not fall back into darkness.
God's salvific deeds and his laws are inextricably linked together,
for they reveal his activity.

III

GOD AND MAN

The commandments, then, are not dead letters on a page. They
are the living words the Lord has proclaimed to his people. They
cannot be separated from the God who proclaimed them. They
cannot be regarded merely as legal prescriptions. If they are
they will be misconstrued.

It is important to realize that the decalogue did not exist at the
start of Israel's history. Israel was already God's people when he
set down his law. Israel was not just the property of God. Through
the Covenant it became his chosen people, freely consenting to

[3] Marc Chagall, *Glasmalereien für Jerusalem* (Monte Carlo, 1962),
pp. 53–64.

obey his saving rule. The commandments are not the gateway leading into God's community. They are meant to help Israel become aware of its existence as the People of God. The commandments summon the community to reaffirm its decision and to exercise responsibility.[4]

God never acts solely in his own interests. All his actions are directed toward a second party, man, from whom he demands a response. The Hebrew word which we translate as "righteousness" is much richer in meaning. It connotes this mutual relationship between God and man. The righteous or upright man is one whose relationship with God is in order; his life prospers.

In all this, God takes the initiative. His activity, which reveals itself in historical events and commandments, is one of *leading* and accompanying his people.[5] He led his people out of the yoke of slavery in Egypt (Exod. 6, 6–8) and brought them into the promised land. When the people had set foot in Canaan and the divine plan seemed to have achieved its purpose, the concept of "leading" became a technical term for God's saving rulership in history. He goes before his people, like a shepherd leading his flock. The "way", which originally designated the path that God blazed through the desert, becomes a symbol for man's life in general.

Man's proper response to this guidance is to "go along with God", to follow him steadfastly. God's leadership is stressed in our text because the Israelites had some bitter memories of their attempts to evade it. Hardened by his knowledge of life, the father solemnly reminds his son of the divine lesson that was taught during Israel's wanderings in the desert: "As a man disciplines his son, the Lord your God disciplines you" (Deut. 8, 5). The son must ponder and heed the Lord's Word (Deut. 6, 4f.). In short, he must keep the commandments, for man lives by everything that proceeds from the mouth of God (Deut. 8, 3).

That is why there was constant and repeated reference to the

[4] Schreiner, *op. cit.*, pp. 41–45.
[5] Schreiner, "Führung: Thema der Heilsgeschichte im Alten Testament," in *Bibl. Zeitschr.* 5 (1961), pp. 2–18.

historical deeds of God in cultic services. Every seven years the Covenant was reaffirmed in a solemn ceremony at Sichem. And in this ceremony the decalogue was proclaimed once more in a liturgical format. This proclamation was accompanied by formalized blessings and curses, which were meant to impress upon the nation that these laws were not dead letters on paper but commands of a living God. It was not a dispassionate recital of past history. In recalling their history the Israelites consciously placed themselves before God, called upon him, and gave their response to God's summons. They realized that God's revelations had wrought an essential change in the life of the nation, that these events were not simply deeds of the past but ever-present realities.

The proclamation of God's salvific deeds in Deuteronomy 6, 20–25 brings the son into contact with enduring life. It summons him to recognize and acknowledge the saving activity of God. It is an historical event that is past and gone as such; in this respect it must be viewed as history. But as a salvific event, it is ever present.[6]

This explains why the decalogue puts stress on the first commandments, which deal with the person of God.[7] They form, as someone has said, a basic position paper in which the relationship between God and Israel is definitively spelled out. The man who has other gods besides the true God has deprived himself of salvation (prosperity) and life. The true God must be *completely free*, and man has no right to lay hold of him even if his intentions are honorable. That is why men are not permitted to make graven images of him, or to use his name in vain. Such actions represent attempts to impress God into the service of human desires, to transfer the initiative from God to men. For God's summons is not a sometimes thing; his dynamic creative power hangs over man at every moment. He is a jealous God, who manipulates all history (Ezek. 20, 41) and even invades the family household to lay hands on baskets and kneading-troughs (Deut. 28, 5).

[6] M. Noth, "Die Vergegenwärtigung des Alten Testamentes in der Verkündigung," in C. Westermann, *Probleme alttestamentlicher Hermeneutik* (Munich, 1960), pp. 54–68.

[7] Schreiner, *op. cit.*, pp. 67–83.

It is also clear that the decalogue is directed to the people as a community. In our citation the father tells what God did for "us". Hence the "thou" of the commandments ("Thou shalt not . . .") is aimed at Israel as a whole and at the individual member who is inextricably linked to this community. The problem of individual versus community, which is a lively issue today, did not exist in the Old Testament. It is interesting to note that modern man is beginning to turn his attention once again to the question of community relationships. God's revelation has come in for new consideration as man tackles the implications of the fifth commandment for such problems as war and legitimate revolution.

The commandments definitely do not present a code of individualistic ethics. They must be viewed in terms of the relationship between God and man and the relationships between man and man. They are not directed exclusively to the pious; indeed they are primarily aimed at the laity, for it forms the kernel of God's community. Passive obedience, however, is not the proper response to the dynamic God. The Israelites are ransomed captives who have been set free from their chains. They must actively take sides with God in their daily activity.

IV

THE MESSAGE OF THE COMMANDMENTS

This brings us right to the heart of the commandments. The first thing that strikes us is that all, except the third and fourth, are formulated negatively: "Thou shalt *not*." The modern individual, who runs into "forbidden" signs everywhere in daily life, bristles at the thought of encountering similar strictures in the religious sphere. In his relationships with God he wants to act freely and in a more positive way.

In actual fact, however, the prohibitions are only boundary markers that stake out the territory of God's dominion. As a member of the community, the individual already lives within this territory. Here it becomes evident that the commandments are not dealing with theoretical problems in theology; they are trying to forestall the more acute dangers that could crop up among God's people. While these dangers might vary with time and place, they would always tend to disrupt order within the realm of God's authority.

The first commandment, for example, played a significant role in the era of the Deuteronomists. The Canaanite religion was stressing worship of idols and images, and it exuded sensuality. Over against this atmosphere, the first commandment served as a danger sign, reminding the people of God's uniqueness and his special privileges. That particular historical crisis has passed, but the underlying point of the first commandment—God's salvific will and design—is ever valid. Whenever God's place of honor is challenged, whether it be by idols or by a materialist philosophy, the first commandment recalls the proper emphasis.

Behind all the commandments we find the wisdom of experience. Experience teaches us that man likes to *step over the border line*. Adam and Eve, for example, were not content with the fullness of paradise; they went after the forbidden fruit. Modern man in particular tends to lean over the edge, and this frequently poses threats to his very existence.

On the other hand, boundary lines also provide for *free development* within their borders.[8] It is here that we see clearly how much we moderns have to recast our thinking in order to understand the Bible correctly. The Semitic mentality never looks solely at one aspect of a situation; it always tries to see the full picture. Prohibitions merely circumscribe the boundaries within which the individual can exercise his initiative. Within these boundaries the individual is free to improve and solidify the community of God's people. *Goodness can never be hemmed in by limitations.* The preachers who tried to interpret the decalogue in terms of concrete daily life stressed this point. This is clearly evident in Deuteronomy, where the laws are constantly related to their source in God.

[8] Schreiner, *op. cit.,* p. 45.

There is a long history of literary development behind the present form of the decalogue. The laws on keeping the Sabbath and honoring parents represent two typical positive developments. They were incorporated into the decalogue because they touched the very heart of the community and also indicated how the other commandments were to be interpreted. In the post-exilic period, the Sabbath took on decisive importance because it held the nation together on the religious plane. Parents are the original authorities on which the family and the entire community are built; hence they must be honored by their children. This ideal is still upheld in the Arab world today.

The Hebrew word which we (following the Septuagint) translate as "honor" is a religious term with rich meaning. It was used with reference to God, so the idea is that God was to be honored in one's parents.[9] But there is only one way for man to honor God—with his whole heart, his whole soul and his whole strength (Deut. 6, 5). Thus the positive cast of the commandments summons man to do more than just obey secondary precepts; he must strive to be holy, even as God is (Lev. 19, 2). As Jesus put it: "You must be perfect, as your heavenly Father is perfect" (Mt. 5, 48).[10]

The *real man* is the one who has his roots in God's community and in the order he has established, the one whose behavior is marked by goodness and love. As the prophet Micah said: "He has showed you, O man, what is good; and what does the Lord require of you but to do justice, and to love kindness, and to walk humbly with your God?" (Mic. 6, 8).

Of course, these demands can be met in many ways. It all depends on the concrete situation, which brings a particular issue into focus, and on man's ability to get an ever clearer appreciation of God's nature and his will. Many things that were important in the Old Testament have become meaningless for us today. Why? Because external circumstances have changed for one thing; the wandering in the desert and the conquest of the promised land are

[9] G. Han, *De mandato pietatis filialis in decalogo* (Jerusalem, 1961).
[10] Schreiner, *op. cit.*, pp. 115f.

things of the past. But even more importantly, because the coming of Jesus Christ has brought us deeper into the mystery of God.

The decalogue lays down the basic ground rules of human existence, and the New Testament brings them into even sharper focus. Love (Deut. 6, 5) becomes the chief commandment. Concern for the alien resident (Deut. 5, 14) who now is seen as a fellow human being, paves the way for establishing a proper relationship with one's enemies. In an earlier day the attainment of the promised land was closely linked with the keeping of the commandments (Deut. 6, 17ff.). Once it had been occupied, it was taken for granted to a certain extent—as the wording of Deuteronomy 6, 24 might suggest. However, to the extent that it is a "fine land" (Deut. 6, 18) where productivity is unlimited (Deut. 7, 13ff.) and sickness is non-existent (Deut. 7, 15), it is a future ideal; it points toward a deeper knowledge of God and a fulfillment provided by God himself. For this, man must surrender to God's Word and respond with all his being.[11]

V

A LOSS OF FOCUS

The law was closely linked with God's activity in history; it was one component in the order he had set up. After the exile, however, emigrations and immigrations diminished; God's dynamic protection in the broad realm of historical movements seemed to come to rest. Overwhelming emphasis was now placed on the law itself. To be sure, it comes from God and is overseen by him; but now it is viewed as having its own weight and grandeur.[12]

This new development is reflected in the expression, "*the* law", which referred to the whole Pentateuch. People no longer saw its ties with the Covenant, the living relationship of the community to its God. The law, which was once a living thing, became rigid.

[11] H. H. Schmid, "Das Verständnis der Geschichte im Deuteronomium," in *Zeitschr. f. Theol. Kirche* (1967).

[12] M. Noth, "Die Gesetze im Pentateuch," in *Gesammelte Studien zum Alten Testament* (Munich, ³1966), pp. 112–36.

As a result, the whole weight of the law bore down on man's actions. He no longer felt himself to be a member of a larger group. He had to confront the law as a solitary individual; rewards were meted out for its observance, punishments for its non-observance. These notions are alien to the original concept of the law. Originally, blessing came through God's election itself, and only those who left the sphere of God's dominion were cursed.

This outlook is depicted in Psalm 1, which describes the man whose "delight is in the law of the Lord, and on his law he meditates day and night" (Ps. 1, 2). One's attitude toward the law places him in the ranks of the just or in the ranks of sinners. The transgressor, of course, is the dark side of the just man, who makes the latter look all the better. But the just man need not be pharisaical either; he can be a truly upright man, opening his heart to the words of revelation. Undoubtedly, however, many men of that period took a different path.

Now we see why Paul attacked this attitude toward the law. It is a later attitude toward the law, and we mistakenly take it to be the real outlook of the whole Old Testament. In the person of Christ the living relationship between God and the law is reestablished.

We must realize full well that such warped development is not restricted to Judaism. Whenever laws and constitutions are wrenched from their living roots, whenever they become mere tradition, they tend to stultify. The individual who lacks personal initiative, who lacks the courage to respond to God with his whole heart, feels that he is buried in the shadows of the law. Reward and punishment are all that such laws mean to him. Christians must always remember what happened to the course of Judaic law, for they are open to the same danger. Laziness and the desire for security can produce the same results today.

VI

THE NEW TESTAMENT AND THE LAW

The decalogue is valid in the New Testament too. Jesus did not come to eliminate the law but to fulfill it (Mt. 5, 17). When he talks to the rich young man, he first calls his attention to the law. Then he adds: "You lack one thing; go, sell what you have, and give to the poor, and you will have treasure in heaven; and come, follow me" (Mk. 10, 17–21). At the same time, however, he also speaks with authority: "You have heard that it was said to the men of old . . . But *I* say to you . . ." (Mt. 5, 21). He is not the ordinary preacher. He is one who has come with divine authority to fulfill the will of God. He rails against tradition insofar as it made absolutes out of time-conditioned interpretations. He eliminates the emphasis on externals (ritual purification: Mk. 7). He stresses the importance of one's internal attitude, developing ideas that were already suggested in Deuteronomy itself (4, 21). The sermon on the mount does more than explain the decalogue; it traces it back to its original source. In the appearance of Christ (epiphany), God's creative power and his redemption become realities once again. Modern Christians must view the decalogue in their light.

In Paul's letter to Titus we read these words: "For the grace of God has appeared for the salvation of all men, training us to renounce irreligion and worldly passions, and to live sober, upright, and godly lives in this world, awaiting our blessed hope, the appearing of the glory of our great God and Savior Jesus Christ, who gave himself for us to redeem us from all iniquity and to purify for himself a people of his own who are zealous for good deeds" (2, 11–14). Then Paul adds: ". . . when the goodness and loving kindness of God our Savior appeared, he saved us, not because of deeds done by us in righteousness, but in virtue of his own mercy . . ." (3, 4–5).

Human life is couched between the first epiphany of Christ and his second coming. The Christian keeps his gaze focused on the Lord, with whom he comes into living contact through baptism;

and he looks forward to the eschatological kingdom, where the beatitudes will find fulfillment. His life is shaped and formed by grace, which develops a truly religious human being. He is "led out", not from Egypt but from a world that does not bother with God, that is engrossed with sensual desires and ambitions.

Man's response to God's epiphany is embodied in daily works of love. The theology of this Word is a development of Old Testament revelation in the light of Christ. This new form of expression, stemming from Hellenism, seems to have little connection with the Old Testament. But it forcefully underlines the ecumenical character that revelation acquired through Christ.

Heinrich Gross / *Trier, West Germany*

Zion's Redeemer

"And he will come to Zion as redeemer" [1] (Isaiah 59, 20)

One of the axioms of the Israelite faith is that at the end of time, at the end and acme of history, Yahweh will have "his day". Faithful to his Word, the full splendor of his mercy will shine on those who have remained faithful to him. On that day he will bring *salvation* to his own. The day of Yahweh represents a turning point in the course of history. It marks a break with the past and a new beginning, outside of man's calculations, which will perfect and complete man's existence and his present life.

I

ESCHATOLOGY IN THE OLD TESTAMENT

References to the day of Yahweh and the transformation to come run through the whole Old Testament; it is a living issue throughout Old Testament revelation. This day is *associated with*

[1] Scriptural citations are taken from the Revised Standard Version of the Bible. On this same topic, see the following articles and essays by this author: "Ebed Jahwe," in *Lex. Theol. u. Kirche* III, pp. 622–24; "Eschatologie im AT," in *Lex. Theol. u. Kirche* III, pp. 1084–88; "Messias: AT und Jedentum," in *Lex. Theol. und Kirche* VII, pp. 336–39; "Die Entwicklung der atl. Heilshoffnung," in *Trierer Theol. Zeitschr.* 70 (1961), pp. 15–28; "Der Messias im AT," in *Trierer Theol. Zeitschr.* 71 (1962), pp. 154–170; "Die Eschatologie im Alten Bund," in *Anima* 20 (1965), pp. 213–19; "Gottesknecht," in *Bibellexicon* (²Einsiedeln), with extensive bibliographical references.

the end of time and *tied to history*. Thus, eschatology, which was concerned with future events and happenings and those of the last days, was part of *salvation history* and an element in the theology of history. Conversely, the actual history of Israel was tied up with eschatology. Eschatological expectations punctuate the course of revelation's history, confer meaning on it, and lead it toward fulfillment.

Through its attachment to history and its development of eschatology, Israel's revealed religion sharply distinguished itself from surrounding religions. By its emphasis on redemption and future salvation, promised by Yahweh, the unbounded and enduring dominion of God becomes the central theme of revelation. The establishment of this dominion, however, is the work of God alone; no one can arrange it but he. He will bring it about, using the same sovereign power and freedom that created the world and established the covenant.

The religions that surrounded Israel were tied to nature. Fulfillment for them was achieved in the cycle of eternal return. In such a cyclic view, the last member of the chain picks up the first member once again. Here there is no doctrine about the last things, for the fated cycle of return precludes the possibility of genuine history. Good and bad times alternate with each other in magical fashion. By contrast, Israel's revealed religion provides for another type of fulfillment: salvation for God's people in the future, on a fateful day of transformation. Eager expectation for this day punctuates the course of history, and there is no turning back. The pilgrimage to God derives meaning from the *eschaton,* which Yahweh will bring about.

II

THE ORIGINS AND DEVELOPMENT OF OLD
TESTAMENT ESCHATOLOGY

The movement of God's people from promise to fulfillment, which offers even greater promises, was the basis on which Israel developed her eschatology. As her expectations were realized, her longing for God's definitive kingdom was intensified; having seen a part of God's salvific plan and design fulfilled, she became that much more anxious to see his definitive salvation.

God's promise made it clear to his chosen people that it would not be completely fulfilled in the present. At the very beginning of Israel's history, God makes a promise to Abraham, a promise that points toward the future (Gen. 12, 1–3). From this point on, Israel's history is a salvation history oriented toward the future. She lives by the norm of promise and fulfillment.

From the very beginning, Israel's expectations about the end of time were tied up with her general expectations about the future, and they developed from the latter. However, Israel's eschatology did not exist full-blown at the beginning of her history; it developed gradually as Israel experienced God's guidance in history, as she moved from promise to fulfillment. Revelation moved step by step toward the *eschaton,* which lay outside the realm of historical experience. Israel's unique and continuing encounter with her God and his divine revelation became decisive factors for her progress and development through history. Historical achievement and partial fulfillment of broad promises also represented new and more concrete promises; they fed Israel's expectations about what was yet to come. The norm of promise and fulfillment is the driving force which gives rise to Old Testament eschatology and regulates its development.

Running parallel to the divine promise made to Abraham, but on a higher level, is the promise of a homeland for the nation itself. The nation is summoned to journey into a land "flowing with milk and honey" (Exod. 3, 8. 17; 13, 5; *passim*). Like the blessing bestowed on Abraham, Yahweh's pledge to be with his people represents salvation (prosperity and success) from the very first. In fact, the promise actually goes far beyond the fulfillment envisioned and leaves the way open for a loftier type of fulfillment. Eschatology, then, represents a promise that clearly anticipates the fulfillment to come. Hence the distinctive eschatological virtue is hope—that is, faith pointing toward the future (Gen. 15, 16).

Perhaps the development of eschatology can be seen most clearly in the notion of a holy war, a war in which Yahweh annihilates the enemies of his people. Here is the starting point for the notion that God will pass judgment on the enemies of his chosen people. In the course of time Israel distorted this notion of God's judgment on the nations. Focusing on its covenant relationship with Yahweh, it transformed the "day of Yahweh" into a day when Israel would be exalted as an earthly kingdom; Yahweh had to correct Israel's misconception.

Israel came to believe that the day of Yahweh would mark a turning point in history, a day on which she, a small nation, would be given dominion over all the nations of the world. For Israel it would be a day of conquest and universal supremacy; for her enemies it would be a day of merciless judgment and annihilation. The prophet Amos (5, 18–20) tried to dispel these utopian dreams, but this false outlook on the day of Yahweh did not disappear. The concept, with its now distorted connotations, was taken up by the prophets and altered to fit in with the moving flow of salvation history and the people's hopes and expectations for salvation (see Is. 2, 11f.; 13, 6; Jer. 46, 10; Ezek. 7, 19; Jl. 1, 15; 3, 4; Zeph. 1, 14–18; Zech. 14, 1).

III

THE ORIGINS OF MESSIANIC EXPECTATIONS

Although Yahweh disapproved at first, the office of king was introduced into Israel and finally received Yahweh's blessing. With the introduction of this office, we find two lines of development regarding the working out of salvation. On the one hand, full salvation can only be brought about by God himself. The great salvific expectations are fulfilled directly by Yahweh himself, as Isaiah 12, 1–3 attests. However, as revelation developed during the course of time, as Israel's hopes for salvation took a more concrete shape, a new figure entered the picture. This new figure, the Messiah, would mediate between Yahweh and his people in a unique way; it is he who would turn these salvific expectations into reality. The Messiah becomes the bearer of Israel's hopes for salvation; he is to be Yahweh's go-between with the people, the nation's deliverer. This figure will do more than bring a better future to the nation of Israel; he will bring *salvation* to all mankind. He will link mankind with God on all levels.

Since this mediator, who is to bring about God's salvation and his kingdom in the *eschaton,* also represents God at the same time, he becomes part of Israel's expectations about the end of time. Salvation-oriented eschatology now embraces this messianic notion as well. The older concept of salvation and the more concrete notion of the Messiah run alongside each other through the Old Testament, criss-crossing now and then. The older concept might be called "impersonal messianism", since in it God himself brings about salvation directly. This concept is found throughout the whole Old Testament; here the salvation brought about by the Messiah is only part of the overall salvation effected by God himself.

With the development of the messianic notion, man's enduring longing finds a face. By means of this mediator, man comes into closer relationship with his intangible God. Yahweh comes closer to him, and he is elevated toward Yahweh. In a real sense, the Messiah represents man's closer approach to God. He concretizes man's openness to the divine and fully actualizes man's potentialities for obtaining salvation, for this figure who brings salvation must first be filled with salvation himself.

Seen in this light, the Messiah represents the full embodiment of human existence. He shows how man is to open up to God and how man can attain divine salvation. The Messiah, of course, is never regarded as being independent of Yahweh insofar as he is the means of salvation. For the Old Testament, there is no such thing as salvation apart from that which comes as a gift from Yahweh. It is Yahweh who assigns all the Messiah's duties to him. Thus the introduction of the messianic notion does not impair that notion that God alone is the Savior who grants salvation and grace.

IV

ESCHATOLOGY AND MESSIANISM INTERWOVEN[2]

1. *Proto-Eschatology and the Kingly Messiah*

With the institution of kingship in Israel, which God opposed at first, we find the germ of a salvific figure which God made clearer to his people as time went on. When Nathan blesses David (2 Sam. 7, 14ff.), God promises that his throne will be established forever; Psalm 89, 20–38 views this as a covenant made with David. Herein lies the foundation and the seedbed for the concept of the kingly Messiah, the *messianic king of salvation.*

As Psalms 2 and 110 point out, this king will execute judgment on Yahweh's enemies, break the back of the coalition against him, and thus pave the way for Yahweh's salvific intervention. Psalm 72 rounds out the portrait of God's warrior. After the battle is over and judgment has been passed, the messianic king will establish God's kingdom of peace in every corner of the world. He can do this because he has a unique mediatorship between God and the nation. He embodies the longing of his people, is king by God's will, and thus stands close to God. On the day of his enthronement he takes on a new existence, for Yahweh introduces him into his own realm of power (Ps. 2, 7).

And so, by degrees, the image of a future, ideal king is given shape. This king, of course, comes from a line of earthly kings and receives Yahweh's special blessing (see Ps. 89, 27). But he far exceeds the kings of history and, as the kingly Messiah, is empowered to bring about the future salvation of God.

The prophets, Isaiah and Micah in particular, confirm and elaborate what the Psalms have to say about this kingly Messiah. The king whom Isaiah envisions (Is. 9, 1–6; 11, 1–5) is distinct from the Davidic kings by virtue of his extraordinary origins and

[2] Cf. "Zur Offenbarungsentwicklung im AT," in *Gott in Welt* I (Festgabe für K. Rahner) (Freiburg, 1964), pp. 407–22.

birth, and by virtue of the superhuman dominion that he exercises. His bipolarity, his position and place between God and man, is clearly brought out. His distinctiveness resides in the fact that he stands over and above the long line of historical kings from David's seed (see Micah 5, 1–3).

The same prophet who draws a detailed portrait of the messianic mediator, Isaiah, is also the real founder of eschatology. To bring about his salvation, God uses the stages through which his people pass in history. In history Yahweh deals with his people. In history he provisionally fulfills his promise. But the final and definitive time of salvation will occur only at the turning point in history, "the latter days" (Is. 2, 2). The hope that salvation will unfold fully in history is set aside by Isaiah. Salvation will come only *after the historical period* (Is. 2, 2–5). What Amos tried to clarify in negative terms (5, 18–20) is expressed in positive terms by Isaiah. The awaited salvation has not become a vain hope; but it only unfolds gradually and partially in the course of history. The ultimate and full salvation, the time of salvation, will come *after this* (Is. 11, 6–9).

This *proto-eschatology,* in which fulfillment will be brought about at the end of time, is to be achieved by the messianic king. Through his supra-terrestrial role, Israel shares in the full achievement of this future-oriented hope. But it will take place at the end of time, not during the course of history.

2. *Universal Eschatology and the Servant of Yahweh*

With the overthrow of the monarchy and the destruction of the Israelite nation as an independent entity, the exiled people were confronted with new and urgent questions regarding the as yet unfulfilled eschatological promises. The monarchy seemed to be so far in the past that one could not picture some ideal king as the nation's deliverer. The tangible point of contact had been lost. And so, during the Exile, expectations about the great eschatological transformation found expression in a new form.

During this period the chief spokesman for Yahweh, who does not abandon his people. is Deutero-Isaiah. He anxiously looks forward to a comprehensive and total transformation of men and things, indeed of the whole environment (Is. 41, 20; 44, 24; 48, 6f.; 51, 9–11). God will establish his new kingly rule on a totally new creation (note the frequent use of the verb *bārā*). He will set up this kingdom on Zion once again; it will be definitive and all-encompassing (Is. 52, 7). Thus, while the first Isaiah sees the time of salvation coming out of the eschatological turning point in history, the prophet of the Exile can shed the present-oriented envelope surrounding eschatological expectations; he projects this hope, in its totality, onto the end of time. It is then that God's universal kingdom will be created anew and his saving dominion established.

The image of the Messiah who is to introduce this kingdom and bring salvation also undergoes change. Henceforth it is the Servant of Yahweh (*ebed Yahweh*) who, to be sure, does retain some of the royal traits belonging to the kingly Messiah (cf. Is. 42, 1–7; 49, 1–9a; 52, 13—53, 12). His predominant traits, however, are those of an ideal prophet. Like his people, this prophet lives and suffers through the Exile; indeed, he suffers *for* Israel. Peculiar to this Servant, and totally new to the Israelite thought of that period, is his expiatory suffering. Through his prophetic and missionary activity, and through his expiatory suffering, he will bring the new order into reality; and in so doing, he will be the *vicarious* representative of the whole nation. He performs his salvific work by his untiring work as mediator, a mediator who finds himself in the same position as his people.

This is the new message that Yahweh sends to his exiled people. They need only accept this new lot with its sufferings and misery. Then God sends them a savior. Like the nation, he is afflicted; he suffers *for the many* (that is, *for all*) and thus brings salvation to them. Suffering and misery strip away the *hybris* which had infested his people. No longer do they cherish their mistaken notions about the day of Yahweh, dreaming about the subjugation of the nations to Israel.

The silent, Suffering Servant now embodies the hopes of the nation and renews the covenant with God. Not only is he himself the concrete embodiment of his people's expectations for salvation; in him the Covenant actually becomes personified. And he will also be "a light of the nations". In other words, the *eschaton* introduced by him takes on universal dimensions, embracing the countless nations besides Israel and including them in the new salvific order.

This is the new face of the Messiah, shaped during the Exile. The Suffering Servant will introduce universal salvation in the *eschaton*, and Yahweh himself will reign as the definitive king of salvation. This new messianic concept surpasses the temporal and terrestrial order even more than did the ideal king. It goes right to the heart of man, focusing on his situation vis-à-vis God insofar as salvation is concerned. In proclaiming the possibility of salvation for the nations, it is a joyous message that hints at the radically transformed relations which will characterize the *eschaton*.

The expiatory suffering of the Servant indicates an awareness that man by himself is incapable of fulfilling God's will through law. Thus the notion of *radical eschatology* takes root. If God expects to get loyalty from his people, he must rebuild and recreate them from the ground up. He must draw them closer to himself, heart to heart (cf. Jer. 31, 31–34; Ezek. 36, 24–28; Ps. 51, 12–14).

This notion of a totally new creation is also expressed in Ezekiel 37. There is a new future for the nation because God breathes new life into the dead bones of his people. Thus he will incorporate the nation into his kingdom and grant them salvation.

3. *Transcendent Eschatology and the Son of Man*

With the end of the Exile, the return to the promised land, and the establishment of an absolute theocracy, the great turning point seemed to have arrived. The chroniclers do not recognize any eschatology, insofar as it deals with an order outside and beyond the temporal sphere. They try to show that Isaiah's hopes for the future have been realized in the post-exilic restoration. Yahweh will rule from the new temple on Zion. As in the time of the Judges, the definitive theocracy seems to have become a reality.

In truth, however, this "realized eschatology" embodies the de-eschatologizing posture of the chroniclers.[3]

The fictitiousness of "realized eschatology" soon became apparent. The people had returned to the promised land and the temple had been rebuilt as a sign of God's nearness and as the center of cultic worship. Yet the promises of the prophets were not yet fulfilled, and the longings of the people did not subside. Once again the people became aware that fulfillment had not yet come about.

This awareness finds expression in the prophet Haggai (2, 6). His prediction of a cosmic cataclysm gives new impetus to eschatological expectations. Haggai (2, 15–19) and Malachi (3, 5–12) see salvation drawing near, but the voices of other prophets drown them out. Ezekiel (38ff.), Joel (4, 9–17) and Zechariah (13, 7–9) speak about a final, definitive battle that must take place before the *eschaton* breaks into the picture. This battle suggests that the *eschaton* will not suddenly come about with the peaceful return of God's people to a paradisiacal land; it will only come about at the *end* of time, when God establishes a new order for Israel and the world.

The book of Daniel sees world history as a succession of kingdoms; at the end of the line God's definitive kingdom will be established without any help from man (Dan. 2, 34). The four (that is, all) earthly kingdoms are doomed to destruction because of their brutality and their opposition to God. In their place will come the kingdom of Yahweh, descending from heaven. It represents the final and definitive form of fulfillment (Dan. 2, 7; compare Is. 24–27).

The book of Daniel represents the final stone in the development of Old Testament theology and eschatology. Hope for salvation is now placed in the transcendent world of God himself. The Messiah is granted dominion in this world by God himself, and the four earthly kingdoms are abolished (Dan. 7, 10–13).

Now the Messiah is the Son of Man, the third figure to appear

[3] Cf. O. Plöger, *Theokratie und Eschatologie* (Neukirchen, 1959).

in messianic thought. He is the transcendent ruler in God's kingdom, and his appearance on the clouds of heaven reveals him to
be a resident of God's world. His commission to rule may be regarded as a transformation of the older messiah-king motif. The
kingly Messiah is now transported to the latest and highest stage
of Old Testament thought.

In the course of time God seems to move farther and farther
away from his people; he becomes transcendent. With the introduction of the Son of Man, the same thing seems to happen to the
Messiah; he moves farther and farther away from the world of
men. Since he appears on the clouds of heaven, he belongs to
God's world. However, he is still visible to men because he has
the appearance of a man. The expression "like a son of man" re-
duces the transcendent aspect of this Messiah, for it also implies
lowliness (cf. Ezekiel). Thus this messianic image does bring the
Messiah close to man again, picking up the threads of the Suffering Servant image.

The three messianic images discussed here do not exhaust the
messianic themes of the Old Testament. However, they are the
chief embodiments of this awaited figure. We must stress the importance of the prophet image as the bearer of messianic expectations, even though we did mention this in connection with the
Suffering Servant. Even more important, however, is the priestly
image: the high priest as a type of the Messiah.

After the Exile this image took on increasing importance,
especially since the kingly image faded into the background (cf.
Ezek. 44—46; Zech. 3f.). This line of thought is developed
greatly in the Qumran texts. It also extends into the New Testament, and the author of the letter to the Hebrews used it to good
effect in trying to explain the salvific work of Christ.

The incompleteness of the Old Testament and its open-ended
relationship to the New Testament is not readily evident because
there is no overall synthesis of the various messianic images. Each
image presents a partial picture and no more. But the ultimate

purpose of these figures is the same: to make the claims of God's kingdom visible to man; to give them concrete shape and thus contribute to the establishment of God's kingdom.

As representatives of Yahweh, they are to bring God's *judgment and salvation* to men. They are to show men the aim and purpose of earthly life—enduring union with God—and to make this aim a reality. Messianic expectation, with its many and varied aspects, remains the *great hope* which is carried into the New Testament—by the *holy remnant* at least.

The various messianic images can be regarded as an essential part of the development which took place in Old Testament revelation and eschatology. This development was complex, to be sure. The various strands of Old Testament hope for salvation are interwoven with one another in the nation's history, but they cannot be isolated with mathematical exactness nor described *a priori*.

Properly understood, eschatology is not man's projection of the present into the future. It is the light of the future being shed on the present by God. It is a promise and a call to man to live for that future in faith, to help bring about the *eschaton* in which God's full salvation will be bestowed.

Salvador Muñoz Iglesias / *Madrid, Spain*

Old Testament Values Superseded by the New

The Christian of today often asks himself what value the revelation of the Old Testament can have for him. And the manner in which the question is asked presupposes the usual reply: very little, perhaps none.

This way of approaching the question is too pragmatic. One tends to wonder what use the partial revelation of the Old Testament can be when the New by definition contains the fullness of God's revelation, or what force the moral code of the Old Testament can be supposed to have when the New Testament explicitly perfects and corrects the morality of the Old.

The Christian who approaches the Old Testament in this way can only create difficulties for himself. How can he explain, for example, the fact that God should have left his chosen people for so long in ignorance of the doctrine of the Trinity, or of individual reward or punishment after death? How could Yahweh condone divorce, polygamy, or mass extermination of enemies? Add to this the difficulties posed by the findings of modern science in relation to the world view, the conception of the beginnings of history and of its outcome expressed in the Old Testament, and it will be readily understood why the average Christian turns his back on the books of the Old Testament in something akin to alarm and takes refuge in the New for a basis for his faith.

Many would agree with Harnack: "The early Church was quite right to keep the Old Testament in the beginning, but she should have jettisoned it very soon. It was a disaster for the

99

Lutheran reform to keep it in the 16th century. But for Protestantism to cling to it as a canonical document in the 20th century is a sign of religious and ecclesial paralysis." [1]

Without going as far as this, there is no doubt that many Christians would welcome a sort of "expurgated" edition of the Old Testament, retaining everything that seemed still useful and suppressing everything that would seem to have been superseded in the light of the New. Such a purge should clearly not be allowed. But would it not be possible to define in general terms what elements of the Old Testament remain valid and which have been outdated by the New and to what extent?

I

REVELATION AND THE ECONOMY OF SALVATION

First of all, let it be said that the purely pragmatic approach just outlined is not the correct one. The Old Testament is not simply a *Summa* of truths revealed by God. Nor is it just a compendium of moral laws, or even a series of inspired books. It is first and foremost an economy of salvation set in history. It is the saving plan of God who both reveals and realizes himself in history. It is a revelation of what God is, what he does and what he is willing to do, to lead the whole of creation, and man in particular, to its ultimate supernatural goal.

This threefold revelation of God takes place in history, as the *Dogmatic Constitution on Divine Revelation* of Vatican Council II clearly teaches: "This revelation is effected in interrelated actions and words: the works performed by God in the history of salvation point up and confirm the doctrine and the realities expressed by his words; the words proclaim his works and throw light on the mystery contained in them" (n. 2).

---

[1] Harnack, *Das Evangelium von fremden Gott* ([2]1924), p. 217. Various similar statements have been made, of which the most radical is that by E. Faguet, in P. Grelot's *Sens chrétien de l'Ancien Testament* (Tournai, 1962), pp. 75–77.

In other words, God reveals what he is, and teaches us his saving plan through the words of those he sends—prophets and hagiographers—which constitutes an historical fact. But God also puts his saving plan into effect through another series of events and through institutions with a saving purport and value.

These three elements—the words which reveal God's intention and teach norms of conduct, the saving events, and the institutions which in practice apply salvation to men within a determined historical structure—comprise what we call the economy of salvation. In the Old Testament the three elements point toward the saving stage of the time of the Messiah, while already, as now, looking toward the time of eschatological fulfillment.

Therefore, when one questions the validity of the old economy in the age of the new, one should not be thinking only of the conceptual formulations contained in the books that make up the Old Testament, as though it were a *Summa* of more or less universally valid dogmatic and moral propositions. It is a revelation of God and of his plan of salvation made to us in progressive stages. It is a revelation in the process of being made, and at the same time a saving plan in the process of being put into effect.

These two planes—of ideological revelation and saving effectuation—cannot be separated from each other because they exist historically in a state of mutual dependence. The revelation forms part of the saving plan, and the effecting of the saving plan is the central object, the heart, of the revelation. (Sometimes the revelation of what a later stage in the unfolding of the saving plan will bring prophetically precedes its historical embodiment. This happens with the vision of the messianic benefits announced by the Old Testament prophets, and with the eschatological fullness still to come, partially revealed by these same prophets and fully revealed by Christ. Sometimes the opposite happens: the express revelation of the New Testament and the coming of the saving messianic era show what the saving purport and the content of the partial revelations of earlier areas were.) These continual cross-currents between revelation and salvation mean that, when we come to decide what is still valid in the Old Testament and what has been superseded by the New, we cannot separate its verbal content from its effect.

II

STATIC AND DYNAMIC CONSIDERATIONS

There is an important difference between considering this process of revelation and saving action of God in a static form and in a dynamic form. This difference naturally has repercussions on our evaluation of the different stages of this double process. I propose to take two examples, one of a conceptual process and one of an actual process.

If a person with normal sight says to a blind man: "There's an object coming along the road and it's a man, about forty years old, called Fr. Smith, who is the parish priest of St. Mary's in Parkchester," this would be a case of progressive revelation. Each successive phrase adds something to the revelation contained in the preceding one, and the last objectively contains all the preceding ones. Now if I conceive this progressive revelation *dynamically,* all its parts have some value, and there is simply no point in asking if they cease to have value once the speaker has come to an end and the blind man has heard the last phrase. Let us suppose that there were some other blind men standing with the one who listened to the end, but who went off one by one while the speaker was in the course of making his "revelation": the phrases that they heard would lack the full value that they take on once the revelation is complete. But this does not mean that they would not hear anything of authentic value. Only if we consider these successive revelations in a *static* form, as a series of disconnected conceptual affirmations, can we judge them to be invalid because superseded by the last one.

Now for the practical process. An architect wants to build a restaurant in a big city from which the diners can enjoy a panoramic view over the whole city from their seats. It has to be higher than the highest buildings of the city. He will dig deep foundations and build a tall structure with staircases and shafts for elevators. When the building is completed, foundations, supporting structure and restaurant will form a whole. It can never be said that the foundations and supports lack meaning or value within the context of the *dynamic* whole—the carrying out of the architect's plan. They no longer have any isolated existence. They are not independent *static* parts, but are inseparably welded to the unity which is the completed building. But the same cannot be said of the machines and accessories used at the different stages of construction—excavators, scaffolding, cranes, etc. These, once they have served their term of usefulness, are removed.

III

The Different Stages of Saving Revelation and Effect

God could have ordered a unique economy of salvation valid for all time, revealing the totality of his plan and instituting the definitive instruments for putting it into effect right from the beginning. But he preferred to carry out his plan in different stages, each of which represents an advance in the fulfillment of the divine plan over the preceding one: an advance in revelation and a new saving structure for the institutions through which the revelation is put into effect.

1. *The Original Stage*

From the beginning, God raises man to a state of original justification by his gratuitous conferring of praeternatural gifts. Once this privileged situation has been lost through original sin, the second stage begins.

2. *The Natural Law Stage*

This is what St. Paul calls "the times of ignorance" (Acts 17, 30), the times of "divine forbearance" (Rom. 3, 25), the times in which God allowed "all the nations to walk in their own ways" (Acts 14, 16), although "he did not leave himself without witness, for he did good and gave you from heaven rains and fruitful seasons, satisfying your hearts with food and gladness" (Acts 14, 17), so that men might "seek God, in the hope that they might feel after him and find him" (Acts 17, 27). In fact, "when Gentiles who have not the law do by nature what the law requires, they are a law unto themselves, even though they do not have the law. They show that what the law requires is written on their hearts. . . ." (Rom. 2, 14f.). This shows that the saving economy of the natural law remains effective for the pagan world even after God has, with the promise made to Abraham, initiated the third stage.

3. *The Stage of the Promise*

This is characterized by the choice of a people to be the depositary of the messianic promises. Through the descendants of Abraham, God's future intervention in favor of the whole of humanity is first glimpsed. This is a saving time in which everything is tied to the initiative of God and the attitude of obedience on the part of man, expressed through faith. The alliance of Sinai marks the beginning of a new stage.

4. *The Stage of the Written Law*

God establishes a pact with this people he has chosen, to deposit with them his saving promise, and from them will be born the one who is to fulfill the promise of salvation, Jesus. Their state as a community freely chosen and set apart from other nations for this saving purpose constitutes the people of the alliance of Sinai "a holy race and a royal priesthood". To enable them to play their part in the plan of salvation, God gives them a positive law and a set of institutions which, though obviously transitory, are effective at this provisional stage in the saving plan. The moral aspect of this positive law "belongs to the order of the saving plan. Through this, God comes to the help of man to save him from his moral errors; the Word of God is bestowed on mankind to lead it from afar toward healing".[2] The moral aspect of this written law sanctions the natural law of the second stage, and is in its turn sanctioned by the New Testament in the final stage, when Christ comes not to abolish but to fulfill the law (Mt. 5, 17–19), when it will be seen that "he who loves his neighbor has fulfilled the law" (Rom. 13, 8). The laws governing ceremonial (the one sanctuary, the priesthood, worship, sacrifices, the sabbath, holy days, circumcision, ritual practices) and other social institutions (prophecy, wise men) and even political ones (the monarchy) define the structure of the chosen people and help to mold it into the holy community that its provisional mission requires it to be. Eventually the final stage comes.

5. The Messianic Stage

This is the stage of the fulfillment of the promise in Christ and the Church. In Christ God establishes a new economy of salvation which supersedes all the preceding ones. Revelation and salvation are complete—except only for the eschatological fulfillment.

In knowledge of God, of his saving plan and of the rules that should govern the free conduct of man, both the natural law and the partial and mediate revelations of the old economy give way to the complete and immediate revelation of God in Christ. God who "in many and various ways spoke of old to our fathers by the prophets, in these last days has spoken to us by a Son" (Heb. 1, 1f.). The great revelation of God is the very fact of the incarnation of the Word and the work of salvation completed by the Word. "No one has ever seen God; the only Son, who is in the bosom of the Father, he has made him known" (Jn. 1, 18). The preaching of Christ has made God known to us and through his Spirit leads us to the fullness of truth (Jn. 16, 13). But the fullness of the eschatological individual perception is still lacking: "Now we see in a mirror dimly, but then face to face. Now I know in part; then I shall understand fully, even as I

[2] Grelot, op. cit., p. 176.

have been fully understood" (1 Cor. 13, 12). "It does not yet appear what we shall be, but we know that when he appears we shall be like him, for we shall see him as he is" (1 Jn. 3, 2).

The sacrifice of Christ, in the actual order of salvation, reconciles humanity to God. His resurrection and ascension are the first fruits of the definitive salvation that will be effected when Christ comes again to raise up the dead and hand over his kingdom to the Father. The actual application of this salvation to each individual is brought about through the incorporation of each individual into Christ through faith and the sacraments administered by the Church as channels of grace.

IV

WHAT HAS BEEN SUPERSEDED IN THE OLD ECONOMIES OF SALVATION

The new and definitive stage of salvation inaugurated with the redemption through Christ requires that many worn-out elements of the old stages will be abandoned. St. Paul makes this quite clear: "If anyone is in Christ, he is a new creation; the old has passed away; behold, the new has come. All this is from God, who through Christ reconciled us to himself and gave us the ministry of reconciliation; that is, God was in Christ reconciling the world to himself, not counting their trespasses against him, and entrusting to us the message of reconciliation" (2 Cor. 5, 17–19). This radical change is brought about by two factors: the reconciliation in Christ and the handing over of new instruments of salvation to the Church.

In general terms one could say that the new stage *crowns* all the revelation made known and the salvation put into effect by God in the preceding stages. Final salvation will be the same for those who lived before Christ as for those who will live after Christ. But those who come after him possess a knowledge that was denied to those who came before him, and this knowledge must of course be used to correct the deficiencies of earlier knowledge. Even without the complete revelation of the eschaton, we possess certain means of salvation which in this new stage supersede earlier ones.

The old alliance, being a shadow of the new (Col. 2, 17; Heb. 8, 5; 10, 1) or a copy of what is to come (Heb. 8, 5; 9, 23f.), will disappear and be replaced by a new one (Heb. 8, 6–13). The priesthood and the sacrifices of the old law, unable to sanctify man and please God (Heb. 9, 9; 10, 1–4. 11), are dispensed with and replaced by the infinite value of praise and the perfect satisfaction present in the sacrifice of Christ (Heb. 9, 11–15; 10, 5–10. 12–14). The written law, which dictated the norms governing sin, but could not fulfill the just requirements of the law in us (Rom. 3, 20; 8, 3) and so could not justify (Gal. 2, 16; 3, 11), is also "set aside because of its weakness (Heb. 7, 18) and replaced by the grace and truth which come through Christ (Jn. 1, 17) and which give effective strength to our actions.

God's manner of proceeding with the chosen people of the Old Testament shows us the constant elements of his saving actions in the messianic stage that follows. St. Paul rightly insists on the fact that all this was written in the Old Testament for our instruction (Rom. 4, 23, etc.). But there are important points of difference.

Under the old dispensation, the infidelity of the Hebrew people meant the breaking of the alliance of Sinai (Jer. 31, 32; Heb. 8, 6–13); the new alliance of the messianic era can never be broken (Is. 54, 10; 55, 3; 59, 21; 61, 8; Jer. 31, 35–57; 33, 14–26; Ez. 37, 26).

The old alliance was made with the Hebrew people and no other, and this will give way to one that embraces all mankind without distinction of race (Rom. 2, 10f.; 3, 29f.; 4, 11f.; 10, 12f.; Gal. 3, 28f.; 5, 6; 6, 15) through the redemption in Christ. This alters the orientation of salvation and the internal dynamic of both economies. The alliance of Sinai tended to keep the people of the promise apart; the Gospel alliance, on the other hand, is an economy of incarnation, of involvement in the world, as the parables of the light (Mt. 5, 14–17), the salt (Mt. 5, 13), and the leaven (Mt. 13, 33) clearly indicate. Consequently, all those ritual practices of the old law designed to maintain the particularity and apartness of the chosen people are set aside and lose their saving value. There is no more distinction between clean and unclean foods (Acts 10, 15; 11, 9; Heb. 9, 10); physical descent from Abraham is no longer a criterion for membership of the People of God (Lk. 3, 8; Gal. 3, 7), nor is the rite of circumcision (Rom. 4, 9–12; Gal. 3, 26–29; 5, 6; 6, 15).

Further still, the spiritual character of the new People of God means that it has no need to maintain the religious institutions (such as the one sanctuary), or temporal and political ones (such as the monarchy), which under the dispensation of Sinai actually delineated the character of the chosen people. Thus the medieval attempt to see the empire as a reflection of the theocratic structure of Israel was undoubtedly an error. The messianic kingdom is not of this world. (This is not to say that aspects of the relationship between God and the theocracy of Israel cannot or should not be considered still applicable to the People of God under the new alliance.)[3]

V

WHAT IS CLEAR AND WHAT REMAINS OBSCURE

The principles laid down in what has gone before suggest some clear conclusions, but many things remain obscure.

1. It is clear that the reconciliation of humanity to God in Christ and the institution of the Church as the means or instrument of universal salvation completely fulfill the saving plan of

[3] Cf. S. Muñoz Iglesias, "La condenación profética de la política de pactos y su vigencia para el Pueblo del N.T.," in *Estudios Biblicos* 25 (1966), pp. 41–73.

God and establish a new economy which replaces the provisional saving institutions of the earlier stages with new ones of lasting value.

2. It is clear that the partial revelations of the Old Testament must, in the light of the complete revelation of the New, be considered as previous stages.

3. It is clear that the law of charity perfects the written law of the Old Testament, just as this, in its moral aspects, sanctioned and in general terms perfected the natural law.

4. Certain dispensations from natural law, granted by God in the written law—polygamy, divorce, and perhaps the extermination of enemies who opposed the progress of the chosen people, for example—are authoritatively removed by Christ in the final stage.

Nevertheless, one is still left without a satisfactory explanation of the religious ignorance and moral imperfections apparently sanctioned by the inspired books of the Old Testament. The answer must lie in a consideration of their positive aspects, and in bearing in mind the educative intention of God: through the inspired writings he was not so much upholding errors as leaving evidence of the imperfect beginnings of mankind—mankind onto which God was projecting his marvelous plan of raising up and saving.

Another point that remains doubtful is the continued validity of the old economies, as particular means of salvation, for those who have not yet come to perceive the proclamation of the new with convincing clarity. What St. Paul says of those who lived by the lights of the natural law during the duration of the law written for the Hebrew people would seem to be legitimately capable of extension to the pagans of good faith of our own day. Certainly the perspective of positive salvation has changed—then it was directed to Israel alone, now it embraces the whole of humanity—but invincible ignorance is an artificial and subjective question compared to the objective disposition of God.

Perhaps the same should be said by analogy of the Jews, who

through no fault of their own, have not come to discover the establishment of a new divine economy. Why should the instruments of salvation established for them by God in the provisional stages not remain valid *for them* now?

God has not ordained that we should have an answer to everything. But he has required us to accept his definitive plan of salvation, and to believe in his wish that all men should be saved.

Hilaire Duesberg, O.S.B./*Maredsous, Belgium*

He Opened Their Minds
To Understand the Scriptures

"These are my words which I spoke to you,
while I was still with you, that everything
written about me in the law of Moses and
the prophets and the psalms must be fulfilled." Then he opened their minds to
understand the scriptures (Lk. 24, 44–45).

This text is primary if we are to seat Christian doctrine on its scriptural bases (cf. Lk. 24, 25–27; Acts 3, 18; 13, 2–3; Jn. 5, 39. 46). It is the last and supreme lesson (vv. 44–48) the Master gave his disciples. It furnishes the kerygmatic theme with which the apostles were charged, at the same time that they were commanded to give full assent to the continuing interpretation that Jesus gave the scriptures. It ends with these words of investiture: "You shall be my witnesses" (cf. Acts 1, 8).

I

JESUS AS OBJECT OF THE SCRIPTURES

"These are my words which I spoke to you." It is known that in several encounters Jesus stated frankly that he was the object of Scripture. He took the risk at the very beginning in the synagogue at Nazareth by announcing, concerning Isaiah 61, 1–2, that this passage referred to him expressly, and consequently that this prophecy was about to be fulfilled (Lk. 4, 16–22). The scandal he caused no doubt made him more circumspect. If he replied openly to Caiphas that he was the Messiah and the Son of God (Mt. 26, 64; Mk. 14, 62; Lk. 22, 67–69), it was because he was about to be delivered from his enemies by death. To his own people, the title of Messiah was explosive, and it was better to admit to less than to risk being misunderstood. However, his enemies needed the scandalous idea that Jesus gave of himself— an idea which they worked to spread—while the disciples suspected the mystery without succeeding in formulating it clearly (cf. Mk. 8, 27–30; Lk. 19, 18–21; Mt. 16, 13–20).

"Everything written about me . . . must be fulfilled." Never has a hero in Scripture dared to present himself in this way. The episode at Nazareth demonstrated its dangerous singularity. The Eleven were able to accept it because they had just lived through the experience of the death and resurrection of Jesus; he was henceforth justified by his Father and glorified—"being still among you," he said, to show that he would not henceforth be greater simply because he would be at a distance from them, or because of his death, but by his new condition as conqueror of the tomb and of hell.

This lesson of Sunday exegesis has for its first effect the definite discarding from the teaching of the Church of all temptation to Marcionism. The Old Testament, in the thought of Jesus, was Scripture. To rediscover something there is to understand it in its essentials.

All writing is fixation of thought; the scriptures are words of God, eternal thoughts of God incarnated in the language of man for the salvation of men. Who would have, then, the audacity to change any of it, except God himself, and can we suppose that he would be faithful to himself if he contradicted any of his teaching and made a liar of himself? No! But it is fitting that he should intensify the light of the truths he teaches, as our eyes become better able to support it. Scripture is a progressive pedagogy. In the Law, for example, there is a base of theological virtues which gives life to the precise and gloomy decisions of primary justice.

There is much charity. The love of God, like that of men, does not remain in a precise milieu; it is excessive, and leads strict justice toward the slopes of the Mount of Beatitudes.

The breath of the Spirit unchains prophecy. All Scripture is prophetic because it is expectant, because it prescribes vigilance, because it demands the sincere confrontation of actions imposed by the Law with the feelings of the heart.

Prophets will be untimely because they move in the eternal. Defeatists, because they oppose the crafty projects of politics which are inclined to do without Yahweh (Is. 7, 10–13). Irritants, because they condemn trade in general, luxury, drunken revels, and they ask for an accounting of the blood of Naboth.

All through sacred history, the scriptures have been open to the *aggiornamento* which renews the covenants and clears the ground of institutions as decrepit as they are venerable. Now the decisive *aggiornamento* is the incarnation of the Word. Saint John in his Prologue puts it above creation. "In the beginning, God created heaven and earth," says Genesis. "In the beginning was the Word . . . by whom all things were made." The darkness is closed to the inextinguishable light, and the world has not received the Word. Then "the Word became flesh . . . and we have seen his glory"; creation has known a new springtime. "Jesus of Nazareth . . . he who is spoken of in the Law of Moses, and the prophets, we have found him" (Jn. 1, 45).

Monotheism, painfully inculcated in our fathers, remains intact, but Emmanuel—God with us—takes on a realistic meaning that infinitely surpasses the one which Isaiah attributed to him and that was no more than a stepping stone in the building of divine condescension. Emmanuel teaches us to distinguish, in the midst of divine unity, the collegial life of the Father, the Son and the Holy Spirit, equal in all things, eternal contemporaries, enjoying equally a single and identical happiness, cooperating in the work of munificence that we call creation. The Son gives witness to the Father whom he reveals, and the Son gives witness to the Father who sends him, just as the Father and the Son will send the Spirit, gift supreme, irrefutable witness. Thus our knowledge of God, through our experience of Jesus, is increased and diversified before the spectacle of the acting Trinity, distributing their roles in order to raise us to themselves. Jesus Christ is thus both man and God, and this duality constitutes only a single being.

II

How Did Jesus See Himself?

Jesus was a man of flesh and bone, born of a woman, and not a phantom. Luke reported on two occasions his normal and harmonious growth "in wisdom, in stature and in grace before God and before men" (2, 52; 2, 40; cf. 1, 80). He acquired strength, charm and knowledge; this was the fruit of his docility toward his parents (2, 51) who carefully observed his behavior from the first, and his progress (2, 19. 51).

But the profound psychology of this nature intimately united to the Son of God is inaccessible to our curiosity. We are able to glimpse it, and to sketch a dim landscape on which shines only "the obscure brightness that falls from the stars", but in which the rising sun will reveal the exact relationship of lines and planes.

How did the marvelous humanity of our Savior accord with the divine being which seized it and by which it lived? The problem surpasses our capability. We can testify to the fruits of this supernatural union, but its mechanism escapes us.

We must be content with what the evangelists tell us about the attitudes of Jesus when faced with the events which they lived through with him. This is a good deal, because these good men observed him closely, and they talked about what went on with a rude frankness that confessed plainly their misunderstandings or their slowness to grasp the Master's intentions. More than once he surprised and dismayed them.

It is best to read the gospels and to let the words and the actions of Jesus penetrate the heart. The Man-God is the perfect model of the Father "whom no one has ever seen" but of whom "the only Son who is in the bosom of the Father has told [us]" and the example for men who are filially united to him.

He is *par excellence* the sacramental sign of the divine presence in the world. What we know of his human nature, so rich in supernatural energies, assures us that the instrument forged by the three divine Persons for the incarnation of the Word is perfect. It is in the order conceived by them to attribute to him the use of resources which qualified Jesus to accomplish his mission, except for this: that the will of his Father, expressed by apparently fortuitous circumstances, was his beacon light. Daily life was significant to him. His visions of eternity did not inspire in him contempt of the temporal, and that was right because he came to perfect the work of the creator by inserting the supernatural in its highest power into the temporal.

Jesus must have known the Bible because he knew that it spoke of him. He had learned to read under the care of his parents; he heard it preached in the synagogue; he prayed the psalms at the familial hearth and with the community. What the gospels tell us of his preaching and of his disputes with the learned men shows that he knew it well, and that it was always present to his spirit. He lived with the Bible, and it lived with him. Scripture pointed out to him the way to go if he would walk without stumbling in the presence of God, and revealed to him the face of his creator.

He was not a scholar. If he attended the village school, he did not carry his studies farther. People did not hesitate to point this out (Jn. 7, 15). An error in doctrine in his discourses would not have been a surprise. They hoped for it, and lacking something better, attributed errors to him so that they might have grounds to accuse him (Mt. 26, 59–63; Mk. 14, 55–59; Jn. 18, 19–22). We might say that he based his approach on the role of the prophets.

When did he discover that Scripture was being accomplished in him? He had always known it, just as he had always known who he was. Son of God from the very first instant, he always behaved as such, just as naturally as we ourselves behave as sons of men. There is no hiatus of a conversion anywhere in the gospels, nor even an appeal for a prophetic vocation such as those heard by so many prophets and which change their whole lives. The manifestations of his baptism and transfiguration constitute not a new investiture, but a declaration from the Father for the use of witnesses, and not of Christ (Jn. 1, 29–34; Mt. 17, 5; Mk. 9, 7; Lk. 9, 35). He conducted himself continually as the Son of God, and not by fits and starts. His human experiences multiplied; his memory registered them; his awareness of those who surrounded him, judged him, contradicted him, became more penetrating; his reading of the holy books and the reflection this gave rise to were not bookish. He discarded the brambles of the "letter that kills" in order to draw out the living synthesis.

His christological exegesis is not his invention, but he received it and it is thus that he discovered it, sooner or later, with more or less clarity, perfect at each instant for the use that he was to make of it, but always perfectible because, on the one hand, Scripture is inexhaustible (Sir. 24, 29) and, on the other, the capacity of Christ was without limit, as was his docility (Jn. 8, 29).

III

JESUS, THE SOURCE OF A RENEWED OLD TESTAMENT

From preaching to controversies, from the Sermon on the Mount to the parables, he gradually built up a *corpus* of the inspired texts of which he was the hidden object. Abraham, Moses, David, the Servant of Yahweh and the psalmists grouped themselves around him, forming a procession of sketches of the masterpiece which he would realize: God made man, Man-God. It is thus that the new Adam is unthinkable without the old; without Abraham or David, Jesus of Nazareth was without ancestors; without Jeremiah, Job or the Servant, his sufferings and even his resurrection are hard to explain, as are much of his dialectic and his rhetoric, which derive from Scripture. By the use he made of it, he is at the source of Christian preaching of a renewed Old Testament.

Leaving aside the specifically kerygmatic use of Scripture found throughout the New Testament, following the method originated by the Master, I propose to discuss: (1) the subject of the prayer of Jesus and the use that he made personally of the psalms; (2) how he substituted his "me" for that of the psalmists and (3) what use the liturgy has made of this; (4) how, finally, the psalter makes an inexhaustible repertoire for the personal piety of the Christian.

1. The life of Jesus was nothing but a prayer, because he never interrupted his conversation with the Father, even when he was addressing the crowds or performing some act of healing. The Father was present to his consciousness which was attentive to render him this witness.

At certain moments, Jesus showed his prayer—by his gestures, when he raised his eyes toward heaven, when he prostrated himself with his face against the earth at Gethsemani. These were familiar attitudes to the psalmists. It is necessary to add the movements that he made together with the crowd in liturgical assemblies. Finally, Jesus prayed in a loud voice, before witnesses, in particular circumstances such as the raising of Lazarus from the dead, or with his disciples—for example, at the time of meals.

Why did he who praised praying in secret (Mt. 6, 5–6) give himself over to a usage whose drawbacks he denounced (Mt. 6, 7–8)? He did not do so, however, until he furnished a formula to his disciples, the Our Father (Mt. 6, 9–13; Lk. 11, 2–4). To teach them to recite it, and to help them memorize it, he certainly had to repeat it with them. According to Luke (11, 1) one of the disciples asked him to teach them to pray "as John taught his disciples". Was he not the teacher of these men he had called to follow him, and what more natural, in forming them in prayer, than to make it in common with them? The Man-God thus gave the example of an essential manifestation to the community: vocal prayer.

This met the needs of human nature—to praise God, to call for his help when in distress, to thank him for his blessings. Could the soul of Jesus remain insensible to the favors which his Father spread through creation, to his continual intervention in the struggle which the elect underwent in order to respond to their vocation? The author of the Epistle to the Hebrews (2, 10–13) presents him to us as the leader of those whom he has redeemed, and he quotes in this connection the author of Psalm 22 (v. 23) who ends his lamentation by predicting the dawn of happy days, propitious to the action of graces: "[In that moment] I will announce your name to my brothers. I will sing of you in the midst of the assembly." The life of Jesus was a communication of graces, among which prayer in common took first rank, and at which he promised always to preside (Mt. 18, 20).

2. Jesus prayed in psalms. He liked the rhythm, the poetry, the religious depth of these songs. His soul expressed itself naturally in his maternal language (Hebrew or Aramaic?). He found there the right expression of his fervor, the resources springing up from the earth and the evocation of David, of Jerusalem and of the Temple, which touched him to the quick. How many times in his life had he sung the *Hallel,* a group of psalms (113 to 118) which were intoned at the paschal meal? The last time that he recited it together with his own was on the eve of his death, assassinated by legal sentence. He was singing: "I will not die, but I will live!" and he saluted the coming day, cause of our common joy: "Behold the day that the Lord has made—may it be joy and happiness for us" (Ps. 119, 27. 34). Could he have imagined in this hour what awaited him and not found in these two verses an assured feeling of hope beyond proof? It was the same when he passed around the eucharistic cup at the end of the meal—could he be disturbed over this expression of gratitude: "What shall I render to the Lord for all his bounty to me? I will lift up the cup of salvation and call on the name of the Lord" (Ps. 116, 12–13)? In this affecting moment, was not his soul transported by the feeling of imminent danger together with the certainty of final triumph?

This psalm was not written originally with the Last Supper in mind; it served to express the feeling of numerous faithful, but at this hour was it not a fortuitous coincidence? And could the psalmist complain of seeing his eucharist confiscated by Jesus? No! Christ gave supreme meaning to all the religious aspirations of writers who preceded him and whom he recapitulated. He sealed their plaints with his blood and their joys in those of the resurrection because, more excellent than the angels, superior to Moses the faithful servant, in the quality of Son, he set off in high relief the religion that announced him and that attained its apogee through him.

Jesus, in appropriating to the circumstances of his life the paschal *Hallel,* was only applying a general law on the good use of pious formulas. One can use them again with intelligence and feeling only by giving them a personal trial. Each request of the Our Father, to be sincere on our lips, requires us to make the effort to fix the eyes of the spirit on whatever concrete need corresponds to it at that instant in our life. This accommodation is indispensable; without it we merely parrot words. This is the unique means of avoiding the mechanical purring of a windmill when we are at prayer. Besides, we will recite much less of the Our Father the more intensely we think of it.

In the case of Christ, there was better than accommodation: there was realization. Thus was uttered the great cry from the cross: "Father, into thy hands I commit my spirit" (Lk. 23, 46; Ps. 31, 6) or this plaint drawn from Psalm 22 (v. 2): "My God, my God, why hast thou forsaken me?", the poignant lamentation of a persecuted one from whom everyone turns away except for maddened enemies. God has put himself at a distance; he no longer responds. Nevertheless this cry is not one of despair: the question proves sufficiently that it asks for a response.

3. Sacred liturgy is the celebration of the mysteries of salvation organized by the Church, the servant and purveyor of resources left to man by the Master and enriched by the gifts of the Spirit.

The primitive tufa of the mystery is the unfathomable charity of God who created the world freely, without thereby adding anything to his glory or to his happiness. Faithful to men, he would redeem them from their sins. He would use the ministry of his Son who would free them by love—"One will hardly die for a righteous man. . . ." (Rom. 5, 7)—and he would rise from the dead to raise us up with him.

Such is the mystery of our hope. It is the raw material of the liturgy. It is used to bring to life the application of the sacraments, the legacy of Christ, where the most humble material elements, under the influence of a supernatural chemistry, become visible and efficient instruments of grace: baptism, the eucharist, penance, holy orders, marriage.

The Church solemnizes the sacraments and their administration. The central point of the liturgy is the Mass, which is at the same time the service of worship rendered to God the Father by Jesus Christ our Lord, and the service of the community which is shaped there by participating in the eucharist and in hearing the Word. The liturgy is a sight for the eyes and a hearing for the ears to instruct the faithful and let them relive the memorial of the Lord.

As for the words, from where are they drawn, if not from the scriptures? By what method, if not that of Christ Jesus? He gave us the example, to the point of substituting himself for the psalmists. For the needs of her liturgy, the Church is careful about texts to be spoken and texts to be sung, in order to express the doctrine of the mystery evoked. It is from the psalmists, from prophets like Jeremiah, that she will borrow passionate tones to express sadness or hope or joy. Thus was built an immense repertoire, with clever applications, to give the feelings of the Lord Jesus.[1]

4. It is difficult to apply the personal piety of the psalter in

[1] Briefly, we might return to pp. 140–49 of *Jesus, Prophet and Doctor of the Law* (coll. *Bible and Christian Life*) (1955), chapter 6: "The Prayer of Jesus"—where are explained Psalms 31, 6 and 22, 2, as well as Psalms 35, 19; 69, 5; 110, 1; 118, 22—and, in the same book, the study of Masses at Passiontide where the Old Testament texts are placed by the Church into the mouth of the Lord (pp. 149–86).

our age. We must hope that the faithful will receive in the next twenty or thirty years a scriptural formation which will familiarize them with the content of the rhetoric and religion of the psalms which presently are expressed in an archaic manner that makes them difficult to assimilate.

Meanwhile, it is in meeting the psalms during the course of the liturgical year—in the assemblies, at Mass or at other functions—that the faithful, not to speak of ecclesiastics, will most surely familiarize themselves if they are persuaded that they will encounter Jesus throughout Scripture. If they take the trouble to find him again in the preaching of the New Testament, they will lose their shyness little by little with the doctrine of the Lord, and will discover the New Testament in the Old.

PART II
BIBLIOGRAPHICAL
SURVEY

Joseph Coppens / *Louvain, Belgium*

Levels of Meaning in the Bible

The problem concerning the senses of Scripture is not a new one in the Church; it is as old as theological reflection itself. The primitive Christian community found the question posed and solved, in various ways and differing degrees, in Judaism itself; and from Judaism it also inherited the holy books of the old law. Nevertheless, we must acknowledge that this question has received great attention in the past twenty years. Both Protestant and Catholic exegetes have tackled it, especially with regard to the writings of the Old Testament.

The aim of this article is not to make a new and original contribution to the solution of this question. I should simply like to describe the present state of the discussion, particularly as it has developed within Catholic exegesis.[1]

[1] For a bibliography see J. Coppens, *Les Harmonies des deux Testaments,* Tournai 1949;—*Vom christlichen Verständnis des Alten Testaments* (Folia Lovaniensia) (Freiburg in Br., 1952); P. Sansegundo, *Expocion historico-critica del hoy llamado "Sensus plenior" de la Sagrada Escritura* (Avila, 1963); R. E. Brown, "The Sensus Plenior in the Last Ten Years," in *Cath. Bibl. Quart.* 25 (1963), 262–85; H. H. Miskotte, *Letter en Geest: Om het verstaan van het Oud Testament in de Rooms-Katholieke Theologie* (Nijkerk, 1966).

I

THE LITERAL SENSE

Let us start by pointing out something on which present-day exegetes are in general agreement: the first and primary sense of Sacred Scripture, the one which must be isolated first in all its original purity and import, is the literal sense. Without any hesitation or second thoughts, the magisterium has backed up the exegetical specialists on this issue.[2] There is almost unanimous agreement, too, on the philological and historical methods to be used in uncovering this literal sense.

The sacred books present themselves as historico-literary works. They cannot shed this lineage; nor can it be denied that they are human works to a large extent, even though faith tells us that they were composed under divine inspiration. For their interpretation, then, we must use those methods that help us to come as close as possible to the meaning of a work written long ago. A book such as *La methode historique* by Lagrange, once roundly criticized, now stands as a classic, and it has found its way into the ranks of popular paperbacks.[3]

Problems and arguments arise when we try to ascertain whether complementary senses are to be added to the literal sense; whether they, too, can be accepted as valid by the believer, i.e., by Church tradition and exegesis. Note that I said "by the believer"; for all these complementary senses in question are situated in the realm of faith. We are not thinking of some complementary sense on the natural level. It is not as if the author actually wanted to compose an ambiguous and polyvalent work, to veil or hide his real meaning behind the words he used. Nor is it a case of the first and original meaning being deliberately expanded or altered in the course of time to fit some new situation. Here we are looking for meanings that were intended from the very beginning, by

[2] Dogmatic Constitution on Divine Revelation, *Dei Verbum Sacrosanctum Oecumenicum Concilium Vaticanum II; Constitutiones, Decreta, Declarationes,* (Rome, 1966), pp. 423–56.

[3] M. J. Lagrange, *La méthode historique: La Critique biblique et l'Église,* Introduction by R. De Vaux (Foi vivante 31). Paris, 1966.

the principal author, God, primarily, and which were present in the obvious literal sense in some way. How they were present is what one must try to spell out.

We must point out right away that the vast majority of theologians and exegetes are united in their mistrust of allegorical senses. Allegory is a method inherited from Greek thought; it was utilized, in part, to demythologize pagan literature and pagan religious traditions that could no longer be accepted by strict reasoning. We do not intend to summarize the history of allegorical interpretation here, because other authors have undertaken this task and their works provide us with a pretty clear picture.[4]

II

THE TYPICAL SENSE

Exegetes are also in almost total agreement on the existence of a "typical" sense. But this agreement dissolves when they try to define this sense precisely and to determine its values, limits and criteria.

A widely held opinion is that the typological sense involves the foreshadowing (prefiguration) of realities that belong to the messianic and eschatological era and its salvation economy. This foreshadowing is drawn out of historical realities—events, structures, personages—that prepare or announce this era and that find literary expression in the inspired books.[5] Thus the typical sense is figurative by definition. As a general rule,[6] it touches on

[4] J. Pepin, *Mythe et allégorie: Les origines grecques et les contestations judéo-chrétiennes* (Philosophie de l'Esprit), Paris, 1958; J. Wilkinson, *Interpretation and Community* (London, 1963).

[5] Cf. R. Brown, *op. cit.*, 270, n. 42: "Hundreds of years before the Pentateuch was written God may have intended that manna serve as a type of the eucharist, but until that writing there was no typical sense *of Scripture* involving the manna. Of necessity the symbolism in Scripture is literary and linguistic."

[6] Cf. R. Brown, *op. cit.*, 269, n. 40: "We wonder with Bourke if there is always a qualitative difference between the correspondence involved in

the realities to which it is referring only by a transposition of the literal sense.

Some have noted that the typical sense derives from historical realities considered in themselves; that is, apart from their primitive context and in terms of salvation history as a whole. For this reason they have questioned whether the typical sense deserves to be called a scriptural sense. The prevailing opinion is that it does. Those who hold this opinion quite rightly point out that the prefigurative realities are real and significant only because they are presented and given literary form in the Bible text.[7]

Biblical experts are anxious to maintain strict standards for exegesis. They do not want typology to degenerate into "allegorical fantasy",[8] such as that to be found in the older works of St. Eucher[9] and Rabanus Maurus[10] or the modern works of Wilhelm Vischer and Paul Claudel. In their efforts to establish strict criteria, they generally cite two elements: (1) the essential conformity of the type with the object signified; (2) affirmation of this typological correspondence in the writings of the New Testament.[11]

Reliance on the second criterion stems from a theological presupposition regarding the origin of Sacred Scripture. Typological meaning, by definition, depends on divine intentions, that is, on the designs of the Spirit; hence only the organs of the Spirit— the spokesmen for revelation and its authentic interpreters— are capable of telling us the authentic types which have been in-

---

the typical sense and that involved in the sensus plenior (SP). David is a type of Jesus; 'You are my son; this day I have begotten you', which in a literal sense may refer to one of the early Davidic Kings, refers by way of SP to Jesus Christ. What is the qualitative difference between these two correspondences?"

[7] "The sense is in the words which express the object; not in the object expressed by the words," A. Fernàndez. Cf. R. Brown, *op. cit.*, 270, n. 42.

[8] A. Gelin, *Problèmes d'Ancien Testament* (Ronds Points 3), Lyon, 1952, 34. See the example cited by him on page 35.

[9] *Liber formularum spiritualis intelligentiae.*

[10] *Allegoriae in Sacram Scripturam.*

[11] A. Gelin, *op. cit.*, p. 34.

corporated into the course and events of salvation history by divine inspiration.

These two criteria do not seem fully satisfactory to those who have studied the typical sense in recent years. A. Gelin developed this point as early as 1952.[12] New Testament confirmations, he noted, often tend to be equivocal. Sometimes they are true typological exegesis, but sometimes they are allegories or simple allusions like those to be found in rabbinical tradition. Hence he suggested that there was need to look for other criteria that would be more precise and more effective.

When we studied the various senses of Scripture in the past, we brought together the true typological sense and the sensus plenior. The idea was taken up by Benoit. In a 1960 article, he distinguishes three cases: (1) the typical sense without a plenary sense (plenary sense = sensus plenior);[13] (2) the typical sense with a plenary sense;[14] (3) the plenary sense without a typical sense.[15]

When we read this article more closely, we see that the second instance of the typical sense (typical sense with a plenary sense) is verified by the presence of "certain major and privileged words which serve as the vehicle for the sensus plenior".[16] The third case seems to be somewhat fuzzier, for at one point Benoit notes that here too the plenary sense results from typology, "a vast overall typology" from which the texts "receive their plenary sense".[17] Taken by itself, however, this sense cannot strictly be called typical, since it does not involve "the appearance of a new person or event which resumes the old while standing over against it".[18] This is Benoit's explanation for his somewhat vague position on this point.

[12] *Ibid.*, p. 34.
[13] P. Benoit, "La plénitude de sens des Livres Saints," in *Rev. Bibl.* 67 (1960), pp. 161–96, 179.
[14] *Ibid.*, p. 180.
[15] *Ibid.*, p. 182.
[16] *Ibid.*, p. 181.
[17] *Ibid.*, p. 183.
[18] *Ibid.*, p. 183.

In the first case mentioned above, the typical sense is found "without any tinge of sensus plenior". Here Benoit is anxious to avoid the fantasies attached to allegory. He points out that the historical sense, upon which the typical sense is grafted, is not rooted in accidental details; it is rooted in the overall reality which the texts in question offer us. Unfortunately, the article does not spell out a clear, objective criterion for pinpointing this overall reality, this substantial substrate, in the text.[19]

Grelot comes close to the thought of Benoit when he introduces two types of sensus plenior:[20] (1) the pure sensus plenior, where we pass from the pristine literal sense to the sensus plenior by giving added meaning to the vocabulary alone;[21] (2) acquisition of the sensus plenior by joint passage of the figurative realities over to the prefigured reality.[22] This takes place by virtue of the realistic import of symbolic language, which is derived not only from the general laws of analogy but also from the revelatory significance embedded by God himself in the historical experience of Israel.[23]

In an earlier paragraph we noted that it is not easy to find a criterion for isolating the essential substrate of a text, the substrate on which a typical sense might be based. Here the views of Duméry can help us out.[24] Studying the structures of Israelite religious thought, Duméry notes that Judaism is a religion that is not only historical but also typological by its very nature. As Israel sees it, history is revelatory to the extent that it manages to express man's covenant with God; and the people of the Old Testament believed that in their case this was done in a unique and exclusive way. In other words, the whole history of Israel

---

[19] *Ibid.*, p. 180.

[20] P. Grelot, *La Bible, parole de Dieu: Introduction théologique à l'étude de l'Ecriture sainte* (Bibliothèque de théologie: Théologie dogmatique, series I, vol. 5), Paris, 1965, pp 368–91.

[21] *Ibid.*, p. 372.

[22] *Ibid.*, p. 373.

[23] *Ibid.*, p. 374.

[24] *La foi n'est pas un cri*, Tournai 1957, 1959²;—*Phénoménologie et religion: Structures de l'institution chrétienne* (Initiation philosophique, ed. by Jean Lacroix) Paris, 1958.

was qualified to become the instrument and the vehicle of revelation. For all humanity it became the figure, the type, of salvation.

Now in Israel itself, revelation was always concretized in an elite, although this elite did remain in constant communion with the community. That is why the representatives of this elite became types for the masses, providing each generation with models and exemplars. As Israel's history unfolded, these representative types embodied successive stages of awareness, a growing grasp of God's Word. The earlier forerunners ended up having typological significance for their successors. The economy of the Old Law and Sacred Scripture, its chief witness, recorded the successive stages of this experience, imbued them with fuller meaning, and incorporated them into structures of living tradition which were designed to preserve the symbolic value of the original religious experience; thus they made these figures into eloquent types or models. In them the Israelite community could clearly see its own destiny.

These types were not fictional portraits created to exemplify some moral lesson. As Duméry points out, they derive from history where they actually did exist as models, as types. It is true, of course, that the Israelite community sometimes made models out of visionary figures, e.g., Isaiah's man of sorrows and Daniel's Son of Man. But Duméry points out that this prophetic or apocalyptic typologizing ordinarily takes definitive shape only when it is crystallized around some historical messiah. To this we would add that here too we are really dealing with the typologizing of historical situations. The figures in question certainly look toward the ideal Israel of the last days, but they glimpse it as an historical reality that takes its departure from the concrete data of the past.

III

THE SENSUS PLENIOR

Now we must consider the sensus plenior itself. As of the present moment, treatment of this sense is not so clear that it has convinced everyone. This is evident from the fact that we have had difficulty in finding a definition that would satisfy all its proponents. Grelot has taken great pains to examine the extensive literature on this question and to formulate a definition that would serve as a common denominator. On the basis of his work, we might suggest the following definition.

The sensus plenior is "the supernatural depth of the literal sense. It arises from the totality of revelation and, in particular, from the New Testament fulfillment of scriptural texts—to the extent that this meaning was intended by God, the principal author of Scripture, and aimed at by the sacred writer's act of faith. The writer's act of faith may be regarded in itself, or in combination with an accompanying process of prophetic intuition".[25]

Thus we are necessarily dealing with a sense that is in continuity with the original thrust of the biblical texts—with regard to both vocabulary[26] and, even more importantly, theological import.[27]

What arguments are presented most frequently to support the existence of such a plenary sense? To begin with, there is the important statement of St. Paul which distinguishes between the letter and the spirit of Scripture.[28] Then there is the concern of some to provide New Testament and patristic exegesis with a more solid basis than simple accommodation, allegory, or even typology.[29] There is also a desire to justify the way in which the magisterium has utilized certain texts, particularly with regard to Mariology.[30] Closely connected with this is the attempt, motivated by ecumenical interests in large part, to bring tradition

[25] R. Brown, *op. cit.,* pp. 268–69: "Let us apply the term SP to that meaning of his [the author's] text which by normal rules of exegesis would not have been within his clear awareness or intention but which by other criteria we can determine as having been intended by God."

[26] P. Grelot, *op. cit.,* p. 371.

[27] *Ibid.,* p. 371.

[28] 2 Cor. 3, 6; cf. Rom. 2, 29; 7, 6; 2 Cor. 3, 14–18.

[29] Cf. H. Miskotte, *op. cit.,* pp. 85–86.

[30] *Ibid.,* p. 85; cf. R. Laurentin, *La question mariale* (Paris, 1963), p. 47.

back to a simple interpretation of Scripture, so that the notion of the two sources of revelation might be bypassed.[31]

Within the bounds of exegesis itself, various exegetes have resorted to the sensus plenior in order to provide a more solid basis for typological interpretation.[32] Other exegetes have used it to establish a closer connection between prophetic texts of the Old Testament and their fulfillment.[33] Finally, some exegetes hope that in this way they can shed clearer light on the relationship between the various religious themes that form the substance of Old Testament faith and its message.[34]

These arguments have varying degrees of weight. And those who reject them also present arguments of unequal merit. Let me list them in the order of their importance.

First of all, some exegetes point out that the notion of a sensus plenior is a recent addition to theology.[35] Moreover, it is vague and imprecise, so much so that its proponents cannot agree on a term and a definition that is acceptable to all.[36] Such a notion could even be harmful. It could distract the exegetes from their primary task: providing a solid historical and philosophical footing for the authentic literal sense.[37] Moreover, it tends to limit the importance and permanent value of the Old Testament to a few privileged texts where such a sense is present.[38]

---

[31] R. Schutz-M. Thurian, *La parole vivante au Concile: Texte et commentaire de la constitution sur la révélation* (Taizé, 1966), p. 125: "Because Scripture itself is the fruit of living apostolic tradition, it needs the heart of the living apostolic Church to be deciphered . . . Scripture, the fruit of the Church's living tradition and of the Holy Spirit, must be read and interpreted in the life of the Church, in conjunction with tradition, to be *fully* (my italics) grasped with all its meaning and implications."

Cf. M. Thurian, "Un acte oecuménique du Concile: le vote du Schéma sur la Révélation," *Le Monde*, Nov. 14–15, 1965, p. 10: "The Bible is not a code of law that completely exhausts the meaning of revealed truth; the correct interpretation of the Church, tradition, is needed if we are to discover the plenary sense of Scripture."

[32] Cf. P. Benoit, *op. cit.*, pp. 180–82.

[33] Cf. H. Miskotte, *op. cit.*, pp. 85–86.

[34] Cf. P. Benoit, *op. cit.*, pp. 192–93.

[35] Cf. P. Bellet, cited in P. Benoit, *op. cit.*, p. 194, n. 1.

[36] Cf. J. L. McKenzie, cited in H. Miskotte, *op. cit.*, p. 90.

[37] *Ibid.*, p. 30. Cf. R. Brown, *op. cit.*, pp. 262, 281.

[38] H. Miskotte, *op. cit.*, p. 185.

In addition to all this, the sensus plenior seems to be totally superfluous, for two reasons. (1) It seems doubtful that it can perform the functions expected of it; non-Catholic exegetes, for the most part, do not discuss it and even some Catholic exegetes reject it.[39] (2) Other methods of investigation and scriptural usage could perform the same function, e.g., investigating the religious values of the Old Testament,[40] or regarding the sacred books as the sacrament of the living presence of the divine Word and the divine Spirit.[41]

Finally, there is the most serious objection. Some assert that the existence of a plenary sense does not jibe with the classic concept of scriptural inspiration, because the sacred writer is viewed as being unaware of it. For the same reason, this notion is not easily reconciled with the general notion of literary work; it attributes to the authors certain meanings which they did not intend to include in their work.[42]

Since these opposing arguments have been much discussed, we are now in a better position to evaluate them. That the notion is relatively new can be debated, but this does not affect its validity.[43] That it still lacks sufficient clarity is obvious enough, but this is understandable since it is now in the process of development.[44] Its alleged harmfulness cannot be proven: its major proponents never cease to point out that the first task of the exegete is always the quest for the literal sense. The sensus plenior depends on the testimony of the sacred books themselves and on their authentic interpreter, the Church's magisterium.[45] Since

[39] R. Brown, op. cit., p. 281: "It is encouraging to see how many names can be added to our list of 1955 (Diss., 96) as supporters of the theory: M. Bourke, Charlier, de la Potterie, Feuillet, Gelin, Giblet, Hessler, Huesman, Kerrigan, Krumholtz, Levie, Michl, Roland Murphy, Nicolau, O'Rourke, Peinador, Siegman, Spicq(?), to name a few." Ibid., p. 281: "Some non-Catholics (Grant, Markus) have shown interest."

[40] Cf. H. Duesberg, Les valeurs chrétiennes de l'Ancien Testament (Maredsous, 1948).

[41] H. Miskotte, op. cit., pp. 196–99.

[42] Cf. R. Bierberg, G. Courtade, J. L. McKenzie, cited in H. Miskotte, op. cit., pp. 90–93.

[43] Cf. P. Benoit, op. cit., p. 194, n. 1.

[44] Cf. R. Brown, op. cit., pp. 268–69.

[45] Ibid., pp. 262, 281.

study of the plenary sense is not the primary or principal task of the exegete, his first preoccupation will always be to shed light on the major highlights and religious values of the Old Covenant.

Insofar as the positive usefulness of the sensus plenior is concerned, no one expects it to eliminate the role of critical exegesis. Its value lies in the realm of faith. Those who view it in this light generally admit that it opens up new perspectives, that it lets us get a better glimpse of the theological harmony between the two Testaments; such harmony would seem to be called for by the fact that the principal author of both is one and the same, as is the underlying salvific plan.[46]

The major difficulty, it seems to me, is the fact that the sensus plenior seems to escape the awareness of the sacred writer. If this is the case, how can the plenary sense depend on the intentions of the sacred writer and on the charism of inspiration (which presupposes the collaboration of a free and sentient instrument)?

One might try to get around this difficulty by transferring the exercise of this charism from the consciousness of the individual writer to the consciousness of the believing community. There is, for example, Karl Rahner's description of the way in which the sacred books originated.[47] If we accept this hypothesis in our examination of the sacred texts, then we would be dealing with a collective consciousness which could and should be richer and more all-embracing than the literal sense of the transcribed words would indicate.

However, this lets us out of the problem a little bit too easily. Moreover, we can and must insist on the fact that we are dealing with inspired authors. They did not compose a work that was purely human; they composed their pieces under God's prompting. Adopting this perspective, we can picture several situations. In the first situation, the sacred writer possessed the charism

46 P. Benoit, op. cit., pp. 192–96.

47 K. Rahner, Ueber die Schrift-inspiration (Freiburg in Br., 1947); cf. R. Brown, op. cit., p. 274, n. 62: "In Prophecy, 127, Benoit is moving toward a wider definition of biblical inspiration that would make writing only one part of the picture"; likewise J. L. McKenzie, "The Social Character of Inspiration," in Cath. Bibl. Quart. 24 (1962), pp. 115–24.

of prophecy or else wrote down an oracle; in other words, he faithfully recorded a prophetically inspired pronouncement. Granting either of these two situations, we can easily say that these texts (deriving ultimately from such a charism) could contain a meaning that went beyond the full religious awareness of those who wrote them, that they could even refer in some way to a future that was far away.[48]

Now suppose that the charism of prophecy does not enter the picture. In this case we are dealing with authors who are moving in the realm of the supernatural and enunciate declarations of faith (*Glaubensaussagen*). And one of the distinctive characteristics of the act of faith is that in its thrust it necessarily goes beyond the explicit import of its assertions. As St. Thomas puts it: "Actus credentis non terminatur ad enuntiabile sed ad rem." [49] The act of faith deepens the awareness of the believer in singular fashion. It allows us to include in this awareness a thrust or an aim which gives the words greater depth of meaning. And this depth of meaning can contain implications and potentialities that will develop only later, in a situation where new believers are involved. In my opinion, this thrust, which is characteristic of the act of faith, can provide the required point of departure for the presence of a sensus plenior.

In the movement of faith, this thrust is not entirely lost to one's awareness. Gelin once called it "a movement toward, an orientation to, a presentiment of, an opening on";[50] in other words, it is an "objective reference" [51] toward realities that are to come, and the act of faith, under the influence of the Spirit, catches an initial though rudimentary glimpse of them.[52]

We might also add that successive rereadings of the sacred

[48] R. Brown, *op. cit.*, p. 276, n. 70: "the General SP, the Typical and Prophetical SP." Cf. *ibid.*, pp. 270–71.

[49] II-II, q.1, a.2, ad 2. Cf. J. Coppens, *Vom christlichen Verständnis* 22.

[50] A. Gelin, *op. cit.*, p. 28.

[51] *Ibid.*, p. 32.

[52] Cf. *ibid.*, p. 19: "an authentic orentation and thrust, a truth *in fieri*"; 22: "a sound journey that is defined by its goal, Christ"; 30: "The Bible is the *libretto* of this journey"; 28: "The movement of its faith unifies its history"; 29–30: "The dialectic which suffuses and sustains this 'situation' is the movement of its faith"; 32: "It is a question of reliving the upward movement of faith from within."

text over the course of time helped to develop, enrich and deepen the initial thrust and its implications.[53] This process was also aided by the insertion of individual texts into larger collections and by the incorporation of the various inspired books into a unique ensemble called the "Canon". The Canon of Sacred Scripture does not represent the simple juxtaposition of various books; it represents the integration of a vast but closely unified ensemble, which presents us with the complete message of the Lord only when it is viewed as a whole.[54]

Finally, let us not forget that even when a rigorous literary critique of some passage does not provide us with a sensus plenior right away, we can have recourse to the figurative import of the text, to its typical sense. As Grelot explains, this procedure may be all that is required to posit and justify the presence of a sensus plenior. In this case we find our way to the sensus plenior "by the joint passage of the figurative realities over to the prefigured reality".[55] "The key to the sensus plenior of scriptural texts, then, is the systematic study of biblical images," and our colleague set down the governing rules in his discussion of the question (pp. 281ff.).

These remarks, which are new to some extent, may help to resolve some of the major theoretical objections to the sensus plenior. But how does all this work out in practice? Some may well object that one of the examples I have presented as the perfect illustration of the sensus plenior—the Marian interpretation of Genesis 3, 15—is hardly convincing.[56]

Rereading my old commentary on this passage, I can readily admit that I may have forced the "Marian import" of this passage. It is not too difficult to discover an eschatological import in it,[57]

[53] R. Brown, op. cit., p. 278, n. 78: "With Coppens we admit an element of newness in the SP."

[54] J. Coppens, "Comment mieux concevoir et énoncer l'inspiration et l'inerrance des Saintes Ecritures," in Nouv. Rev. Theol. 86 (1964), pp. 933–47; Anal. Lov. Bibl. Orient., ser. IV, no. 13, Brussels, 1964.

[55] P. Grelot, op. cit., p. 373.

[56] H. Miskotte, op. cit., p. 151; cf. J. Coppens, "Le protévangile: Un nouvel essai d'exégèse," in Eph. Theol. Lov. 26 (1950), pp. 5–36.

[57] Cf. J. Coppens, "Le prémessianisme vétérotestamentaire," in Aux grands carrefours de la révélation et de l'exégèse de l'Ancien Testament (Recherches bibliques, 8), 173–78, Brussels-Paris, 1966.

and the forecast of a battle that will end in victory.[58] We can even see a victory that ultimately calls for an individual antagonist over against the serpent, who also is individualized at the end of the oracle. But it is not so easy to find, on the same level, the seed of a Marian interpretation. Lambert was satisfied with the simple presence of a typological meaning, and his minimalist interpretation did not run into theological opposition.

In reality, to arrive at some sort of Marian import I had to reason as follows. The text, I noted, talks about a battle between the serpent and the woman. Now verse 15 is oracular, and thus its import goes beyond the immediate context. Since this is so, the "woman" is not simply Eve alone; it designates the whole female sex. Thus the whole female sex is tied up in the battle with the serpent. This being the case, it is only natural that the female sex prosecutes the battle at the same time as the seed, and in the same conditions. Under these conditions it is only fitting that at the final stage, where the seed is individualized, the female sex be associated with the vanquisher in a way that is just as distinctive and individual.

Now since this was my reasoning, it seems that the Marian import no longer rests on a sensus plenior but rather on a typical sense—and a consequent one at that, for a long and complicated reasoning process is involved. A sensus plenior arises only in the Vulgate version. This latter rereading is not inspired, of course. But it does bear witness to the faith of the Church, which rereads an old text and deepens its message on the basis of a long salvation history that it has experienced.

IV

CONCLUSIONS

We have tried to explain the sensus plenior as something which results from prophetic intuition or the thrust of supernatural faith, as enriched over the course of time by a living tradition which

[58] *Ibid.*, pp. 174–76.

serves as its authentic interpreter. Understood in this way, the sensus plenior seems best able to move us beyond the literal sense into the "spirit" of Scripture. Of all the complementary senses, it seems to correspond most closely to this spirit. If this be true, then the sensus plenior measures up to the arguments and expectations voiced in its favor, and it would appear to be an important factor in the elaboration of an Old Testament theology.

The whole notion of such a theology and its methodology has been the subject of many recent discussions. Quite a few authors are now trying to find new ways to bring out the harmony between the two Testaments.[59] It seems we must agree with Benoit's assertion that the discovery of the plenary sense will help us. For now the Bible appears to be a living book, in which successive rereadings and deeper penetrations marked out the stages of a spiritual journey whose goal and orientation was there from the very beginning. As the Hebrew people moved continually toward their final goal, they bore constant witness to their faith. With the help of the life-giving Spirit, they went over the Word of God time and again, plunging deeper into its depths; its full meaning, however, would only come to light at the end of time.

These are the views I would have on the various senses of Scripture. I think we can say this much at the present time. The views expressed blend in with those of many distinguished colleagues. Undoubtedly they will require correction and further development. Hopefully, this article will stimulate others to reexamine the question and develop even better ideas.

[59] J. van der Ploeg, "Une théologie de l'Ancien Testament: este-elle possible?" *Eph. Theol. Lov.*, 1962, 38: 417–34; H. J. Stoebe, "Ueberlegungen zur Theologie des Alten Testaments," in *Gottes Wort und Gottes Land* (Festschrift Hans-Wilhelm Hertzberg) 200–220, Goettingue, 1965; Th. C. Vriezen, "Geloof, Openbaring en geschiedenis in de nieuwste Oud-Testamentische Theologie," *Kerk en theologie*, 1965, 16: 97–113, 210–18; E. Jacob, "Possibilités et limites d'une théologie biblique," *Rev. Hist. Phil. Rel.*, 1966, 46: 116–130.

PART III

DOCUMENTATION
CONCILIUM

Office of the Executive Secretary
Nijmegen, Netherlands

The Role of Sacred Writings in Different Religious Communities

GENERAL OBSERVATIONS

The modern Christian's search for the values of the Old Testament leads, even though indirectly, to an interest in the sacred books of non-Christian religions. What kind of values does a non-Christian believer find in writings which his own religion recognizes and accepts as sacred, worthy of respect, or revelatory? There are indeed other religions than the Christian one which find the norms for their confession and religious practice in their own sacred books.

Historians of religion distinguish various religions by the presence or absence of a sacred book in order to divide them roughly into religions with a written revelation and religions that live by an oral tradition. Without wishing to judge the legitimacy of such a division, we limit this documentation to information about the place occupied by sacred writings in religions with a revelation that are still expanding today.

It is obvious that religions, determined by a written revelation, do not necessarily judge the value of their sacred books by the same norms as Christianity does. The other religions certainly have in general old and venerable texts, and this they have in common with the Christian sacred writings. The present adherents of those religions also examine the ancient texts for their actual bearing on our present situation. This alone shows the importance of being informed about the nature of those sacred books and the part they play within these various religions.

Our purpose is therefore limited. This documentation merely wishes to indicate the relation between a given religion and its sacred writings, and then to ask some experts in these religions to inform us about the values a modern believer discovers in the sacred writings of his religion.

For the first time in the Church's history an ecumenical Council has made a pronouncement about the positive values of non-Christian religions. The *Declaration on the Relation of the Church to Non-Christian Religions* assumes the positive element contained in their sacred writings where it briefly alludes to the religious problems for which these writings offer a solution: "Men expect from the various religions answers to the profound riddles of the human condition, which today, even as of old, deeply stir the hearts of men: What is man? What is the meaning, the aim of our life? What is moral good? What is sin? Whence suffering, and what purpose does it serve? Which is the road to true happiness? What are death, judgment, and retribution after death? What, finally, is that ultimate inexpressible mystery which encompasses our existence: whence do we come, and where are we going?" [1] Hinduism and Buddhism are mentioned explicitly, while Islam and Judaism are given more comprehensive treatment. Vatican Council II in so many words recognizes the oral and religious values to be found in these religions (cf. the *Dogmatic Constitution* on the Church, nn. 15–16). The experience of these religious values was embodied in the sacred books of these various religions. God also reveals himself in this experience.

To the outsider—and here the Christian is an outsider—these

[1] Cf. the *Declaration on the Relation of the Church to Non-Christian Religions,* n. 1 (Paulist Press, 1966), pp. 8–9. For further information, cf. J. C. Hampe, *Die Autorität der Freiheit III* (Munich, 1967); K. Rahner, "Christentum und nicht-christliche Religionen," in *Erklärung über das Verhältnis der Kirche zu den nichtchristlichen Religionen* (Münster, 1967); A. Henry, *Les relations de l'Eglise avec les religions non-chrétiennes* (Paris, 1966).

writings may appear as philosophical speculation, poetic enthusiasm or primitive myths, but to the believer they mean more. He finds there the embodiment of a religious experience which he takes as the norm for his own life. Precisely because the basis of these writings is a genuine religious experience, one cannot take them as merely the product of man himself.[2]

Although an outsider, the Christian also finds something more in these writings and can appreciate them all the more because of his Christian convictions. We believe in the universality of God's will to save. The God of our salvation has all mankind in view, for the Christian God is not a reality who hides himself; he reveals himself and makes himself accessible. He does this in an incomparable manner in Jesus of Nazareth. This does not prevent others from perceiving the same self-revealing God. The absolute character of God's revelation in Jesus does not diminish the authenticity of other religious experiences. Vatican Council II emphasizes both the absolute character of God's revelation in Christ and the genuine character of other revelations (whether we call these "natural revelations" or the "original" revelation is of no importance here): "The Catholic Church rejects nothing that is true and holy in these religions. She regards with sincere reverence those ways of conduct and of life, those precepts and teachings which, though differing in many aspects from the ones she holds and sets forth, nonetheless often reflect a ray of that truth which enlightens all men." [3]

Here Christianity sees itself as the culmination of all divine revelation and appreciates the other revelations insofar as they throw light on, and indirectly clarify, God's absolute revelation in Jesus. It is obvious that the other "revelatory religions" do not

[2] J. Heilsbetz, *Theologische Gründe der nichtchristlichen Religionen* (Freiburg i. B., 1967); E. Cornelis, *Valeurs chrétiennes des religions non-chrétiennes* (Paris, 1965), p. 105.

[3] Cf. the *Declaration on the Relation of the Church to Non-Christian Religions, op. cit.,* n. 2, p. 10. Also cf. C. Moeller, "The Conciliar Declaration on Non-Christian Religions and the Decree on Ecumenism," in *Lumen Vitae* 21 (1966), pp. 4, 506–18; M. van Caster, "Christianity Confronted by Religious Pluralism," *ibid.,* pp. 529–42.

see themselves as referring to Christianity. They consider their own sacred writings as containing the norms and directives for their own faith. When McKenzie speaks, in his article in this volume, of the universal values of the Old Testament revelation, it is already obvious that these universal values are not the specific values of the Old Testament. A "sacred" book is not judged for its high literary quality or its profound philosophy; one appreciates it precisely for its specifically religious values. These religious values may easily lie hidden in more universal values such as freedom, personality, community, etc. When one is aware in some measure of the shifting of accents in the Christian appreciation of the Bible in the course of the centuries,[4] one can understand that a similar process may also have occurred in other religions. Within Christianity Sacred Scripture has been seen as the book of certainty, enlightenment, ethics, piety, infallibility and truth; ultimately, however, all this led to the religious enlightening of man himself and of the world in which he has his place. These shifts in accent are beyond man's control. They are the result of his being conditioned by his culture, his disposition and his development. These accents also determine the kind of questions he will ask himself, what he asks of the sacred book, and what kind of answer he expects to find in the book. These questions will therefore vary from culture to culture, from people to people and from one religion to another. How varied these religious questions may be, and how different the kind of response that is expected, will become clear from the following broad survey of the part the sacred book plays today for the modern believer in some of the great religions of the world.

[4] For a good survey with a bibliography of recent studies (pp. 253–61), cf. John Bright, *The Authority of the Old Testament* (London, 1967).

JEWISH ATTITUDES TOWARD THE BIBLE
Rabbi Arthur Gilbert, New York, N.Y.

"God, Torah and Israel are one" is a classic statement of Jewish conviction. In this day each one of these three concepts is undergoing radical transformation. The most troublesome, however, is the attitude of Jews toward revelation, the sanctity of the Bible and the authority of biblical legislation as interpreted in rabbinic writings.

No one insists that a Jew declare his faith in God. Judaism is a way of life. How the Jew lives and what he will do in acknowledgment of his Jewish heritage are the crucial signs of allegiance. Recent support of Jews everywhere for the State of Israel —whether religiously affiliated or not, whether formerly identified with Jewish causes or not—is evidence, indeed, that an experience of the *peoplehood* of the Jews is the uniting concept in contemporary Jewish life.

The Jew's understanding of God is personal. His experience of peoplehood binds him to other Jews, but his attitude toward Torah *divides* him from other Jews—and, in fact, as we shall see, it remains a source of conflict in his relations with Christians. It is the most provocative theological issue in the Jewish community.

The traditional formulation of Jewish conviction regarding the Bible is to be found in the eighth and ninth principles of Moses Maimonides' well-known "Thirteen Principles of Jewish Faith".[1] Maimonides declared that the Torah has been revealed from heaven. This implies that the whole of the Torah, even as we possess it today, was handed down by Moses; it is all of divine origin. While the real nature of the communication, metaphorically called "speaking", is unknown to everyone except to Moses, in handing down the Torah Moses was like a scribe writing from dictation (Nm. 16, 28). There is no difference between

---

[1] For an excellent discussion of the history of Jewish beliefs based on Maimonides' 13 principles, see Louis Jacobs, *Principles of Jewish Faith* (New York, 1964).

verses like "And Timnah was a concubine" (Gen. 26, 12) and "Hear, O Israel" (Deut. 6, 4). They are all equally of divine origin and belong to the law of God which is perfect, pure, holy and true. He who believes that there is a kernel and a husk in the Bible is considered a renegade.

Maimonides observes, however, that the truth in the Bible is revealed not alone through a literal reading of the Word. The Scripture text calls for understanding and interpretation. The interpretations brought to the traditional law by the rabbis in the Talmud is in like manner to be considered of divine origin.

Finally, in what may have been a defensive response to Christian claims, Maimonides expounds that the law of Moses will never be abrogated. Nothing is to be added to it or taken away from it (Deut. 13, 1).

"Torah-true" Jews, as the Orthodox call themselves, maintain to this very day this very same conviction. In the revealing symposium, "The Condition of Jewish Belief", every Orthodox-identified rabbi agreed, as Dr. Moshe Tendler put it, that "the literal interpretation of the theological doctrine of divine revelation differentiates Torah Judaism from the organized faith communities that have arisen as deviants from the traditional form. . . . Only Moses received the Torah. . . . The later prophets did not simplify or liberalize the Torah. Their sole contribution was to instruct the Jewish nation and exhort them to observe the Torah without modification. . . . The actual words and sentence structure of this divine revelation are recorded in the Pentateuch. . . . The Pentateuch and the oral tradition (Talmud) are equally obligatory on all Jews as the direct instructions of God to his nation Israel".[2]

Rabbi Walter Wurzburger adds: "In view of the fact that all the commandments represent the revealed Word of God, I cannot, insofar as questions of observance are concerned, differentiate among them. In the final analysis, irrespective of the

[2] Commentary Magazine editors, *The Condition of Jewish Belief* (New York, 1966), p. 236. Dr. Tendler is professor of biology at Yeshiva University (Orthodox) and teacher of Talmudic law at its theological school.

doctrinal or ethical content of a given mitzvah, it is observed as a commandment of God, ideally performed out of unconditional love for him as an act of submission to his will." [3]

This traditional view is rejected outright by all conservative and reform rabbis. The degree of emotion with which they counter the traditional belief depends on how human a document they believe the Torah to be. No liberal today rejects biblical criticism, although they are eager to demolish Wellhausen's rigid conception of historical development and overturn his biased judgments.

All liberals agree, too, that there can be no religion without some concept of revelation. For some, however, revelation is an historic divine-human encounter, and for others it is largely a human response to the unknowable. Rabbi Seymour Siegel contends: "The Torah is the result of revelation; it is not identical with it. . . . Both the divine and the human are bound up inexorably in the Torah and cannot be separated or distinguished by means of some formula. The process by which the community of Israel reads the Torah so as to know what is demanded of it in the concrete and historical situation is the process of interpretation called *Midrash*. . . . The process of reevaluating the Mitzvot through interpretation goes on in the living community of the Jewish people. . . . The Mitzvot are the demands of God upon the community, which lives in time, and thus they are subject to change, growth and decay. . . . The community has the right to reinterpret and change its structural obligation in the light of their ability to express our faith and by their power to evoke faith." [4]

For Rabbi Jacob Agus, "the account of divine revelation at Sinai represents not an historical event but a paradigmatic image of the perennial course of revelation". Rabbi Agus continues: "Since revelation can no more be verbal than God can be a physical being, we must regard literalism, or fundamentalism, as

[3] *Ibid.*, p. 276. Rabbi Wurzburger is editor of the Orthodox magazine *Tradition* and rabbi of Shaarei Shamayim Congregation in Toronto.

[4] *Ibid.*, pp. 224–25. Rabbi Siegel is professor of theology at the Jewish Theological Seminary (Conservative) in New York.

the disease of religion. . . . Dogmatism halts the flow of revelation in its phase of surrender to the all-embracing mystery; idolatry stops at one of the way stations along the three currents of freedom." Rabbi Agus explains: "There is idolatry of the intellect in the arrogant affirmations of man's self-sufficiency; idolatrist, too, is the self-righteousness of those who love one or more aspects of the infinite. Worst of all is the self-idolization of community, the public life of which has been [once in the past] enriched by works of beauty and power. To be truly human we must [continually] seek that which is more than human; otherwise, we come to realize [only] fragments of our dynamic self. . . . Since the commandments revealed in Scripture and interpreted in the Talmud are not literally ordained by God, they are subject to change in accord with the best judgments of the organized community." [5]

Rabbi Ira Eisenstein simply declares: "The Torah is a human document reflecting the attempt of its authors to account for the history of the Jewish people." [6] Unlike secularists, however, Rabbi Eisenstein also insists that the values and concepts communicated through Scripture, which remain valid to this time, are not merely the creation of human imagination; they are rather "discoveries"—"partial and tentative glimpses into the true nature of human life. . . ." And, unlike the Orthodox Jew, Rabbi Eisenstein concludes: "A *good* Jew distinguishes between ethical and ritual mitzvot. He selects, interprets and adapts those ethical commandments which seem to him to further justice, freedom and peace. He sets others aside as having been rendered obsolete by the growth of the human spirit."

Thus we see a vast range of attitudes now held in the Jewish community regarding Scripture. In all of these there are certain basic affirmations which also have implications for Jewish-Christian understanding.

[5] *Ibid.*, pp. 10–12. Rabbi Agus is rabbi of Beth-El Congregation (Conservative) in Baltimore, Maryland. Emphasis supplied.

[6] *Ibid.*, pp. 46–47. Rabbi Eisenstein is president of the Jewish Reconstructionist Foundation and editor of *The Reconstructionist.* Emphasis supplied.

The Word of God is revealed and contained in the Hebrew Scripture, but that Word grows, changes and deepens in meaning through the interpretations brought by the rabbis in the Talmud and affirmed by a living community of faith.

A Christian evaluation of Judaism, limited to a reading of the "Old Testament", is a distortion of the Jewish religion. A contrast between "Old Testament" ethics and New Testament ideals is unfair. One must read the New Testament in the context of the rabbinic interpretation of the Hebrew canon.

The uncovering of the literal or historic sense of the biblical Word through higher criticism, archaeological discoveries and scholarly comparative religious studies is only the beginning of the task. More profoundly, we must study how a community of faith lives out its understanding of that Word. The living Bible, therefore, is not the fixed Word of the canon; it is rather the Word as it is given flesh by the contemporary Jewish community. Bible studies limited to libraries will choke on the foul air. Ultimately, the Jew must meet the Christian and together we must see how the Word gives meaning to life. It is in that confrontation between persons and communities that God will be revealed and encountered.

———————◆◀◉▶▶———————

THE KORAN, SACRED BOOK OF ISLAM
Ghulam Bashir, Den Haag, Netherlands

Al-Quran, the Koran, is the sacred book of Islam, from which the believer draws his inspiration. The name itself means recitation and proclamation. But the book has other names, depending on the aspect or function one wants to emphasize. So it is called also *Al-Kitab* (the Perfect Book); *Al-Nur* (the Light); *Al-Hoda* (Guidance); *Al-Zikr* (Exhortation) and *Al-Forquan* (Discernment).

The Koran is not God's first revelation to mankind. He has sent messengers to all peoples, who had to convey God's Word. They came to help man in his search for the creator. An urge toward him stirs in the very depths of our being. Man would not be able to find the way to his ultimate destiny without this light that reaches us through the prophets.

Nature of the Koran

Only the clearly expressed direct revelations which the prophet received during twenty-three years in Mecca and Medina are collected in the sacred Koran. The prophet's visions, his personal opinions and his biography are not contained in the Koran. The text of the Koran is still the same as it was when first revealed by the prophet to mankind. If the Koran has been so carefully preserved it is due to the fact that the prophet had every verse written down under his personal supervision, and he taught his followers to use the same method. His companions showed great zeal in learning the Koran by heart. When Allah's messenger died there were thousands of Muslims, both men and women, who knew the whole Koran by heart. There was nevertheless a fear that sooner or later, consciously or unconsciously, changes would creep into the Koran, and this led to the decision to gather the revelations of the Koran in book form. This labor was entrusted to Zaid bin Sabit. Knowing the whole Koran by heart, he gathered all the verses and chapters (*suras*) in one book, using the then current order.

At the time of Osman, the third "caliph" (successor) of the prophet, the Islam community was already widely dispersed. By Osman's order Zain bin Sabit, together with three other experts, made the necessary copies of the Koran for the various centers of Islam so that they could serve as the standard version for further expansion.

When these copies of the Koran were made, many of the prophet's companions were still alive, among whom was Ali bin Talib, later the fourth caliph. All these men knew the Koran by heart. None of them objected to the codification of the sacred book. We may therefore rest assured that the Koran of today is the same as that preached by the prophet.

For the Muslim the Koran is the principal source of religious guidance. The *Sunnah* (the tradition of the prophet) and *Hadis* (tradition at large) serve as explanation and commentary but are only accepted insofar as they do not conflict with the Koran.

Man's Destiny according to the Koran

The purpose of life on earth is to achieve union with God. According to the Koran (33:37) this is the mandate entrusted by God to us: "We wanted to entrust the heavens, the earth and the mountains with something, but they refused to accept this mandate and were afraid. Man, however, accepted the mandate given to him by God." Because man has accepted this divine commission and tries to act accordingly, he is the summit of creation and deserves recognition. When he fulfills this divine mission he deserves the respect and homage of all other creatures. The Koran conveys this in a dialogue between God and the angels.

This is illustrated by an experience of the prophet. The prophet was taken up to God by the angel Gabriel. Suddenly his guide stopped and told the prophet: "I am not allowed to cross this boundary; you must continue alone until you have reached your destination. The prophet acted accordingly and came into the presence of the All-Powerful." This is part of a long narrative which conveys symbolically how there is no limit to the progress of the spirit of man, and how man can reach a height which is unattainable to any other creature. A Muslim poet put it in these words: "To be man is more than to be angel, but it demands much effort and much labor." Moreover, the Koran warns man that he will go down to the lowest depths if he does not satisfy the demands of the creator (95:5–6).

The Stages of Spiritual Progress

Through its manifold teachings the Koran means to make man capable of fulfilling the purpose of his creation. It leads man to

his ultimate goal by various stages. As long as man obeys his
natural lusts, however, he cannot rise above the level of the
animal. In this stage the Koran teaches man to distinguish between good and evil. When he has learned this, he may call himself "man". From this stage man proceeds to the next which is
that of morality. The Koran lays down the norms required to
reach this second stage: the believer must unite in himself all
good qualities. If he has but one or other good quality, he cannot
yet be considered a "moral man". The believer, therefore, must
not only love truth but understand what this implies. He must
be peaceful, generous to forgive, tolerant, faithful, moderate,
long-suffering and compassionate. He should also realize that
all these good qualities lose their value if not practiced at the
right time and in the right place. The prophet sees his mission
as lifting man to a high level of morality. When man has reached
the stage of morality he is led to the stage of spirituality. The
Koran does this by teaching man that he has been created for
a higher purpose and must constantly tend toward this end. The
believer is made to realize that the value of a deed is determined
by motive and inner disposition. Thus he has to watch constantly
that the motive which inspires the deed remains pure. The believer must act "because of God"; as long he does not realize
this, he has not reached the spiritual stage.

The Believer and the World

The believer's attitude toward his neighbor differs from one
stage to the next. He starts by acting according to the law of
nature: he is good toward the neighbor and expects the other
to respond to his generosity by being grateful. When more ma-
ture, the believer will do good without expecting any return in
kind. But he will still cease doing good when repaid with evil.
At a higher stage the believer will do good and continue to do
so even when repaid with evil. The Koran expresses this as follows (16:19): "Allah surely commands you: 'Adl, Ihsaan and
Itaaizil-Qorba.'" *Adl* means "good for good"; *Ihsaan,* "doing
good without repayment"; *Itaaizil-Qorba,* "to give as between

relatives, as parents give to children". When faced with evil we are inclined to repay in kind, but this a man will only do as long as he is dominated by natural lusts. The believer should be above this. Thus the Koran tells us to forgive the evildoer. The advanced believer will not leave forgiveness or retribution to the dictates of his natural lusts. He is rather concerned with the reform of the evildoer. Therefore, we read in the Koran: "Retribution of evil is similar to the evil itself; but for him who forgives and looks for reform, his reward rests with Allah" (42:41). The truly spiritual man must see to it that his forgiveness and retribution tend toward reform.

The Stages of Faith

For him who is initiated—i.e., starts on the way toward spiritual progress—to believe is at first pure acceptance and trust in what he has come to know as the truth. At this stage he will follow the spiritual laws (*Shariat*) as prescriptions that are necessary for his health of body and soul. He must keep these laws. As he makes progress he is given more insight into the truth. Thus his faith becomes *Irfan* (knowledge) and the *Shariat* becomes the *Tariqat* (the way of life); the indications given by his religion become the way that leads to the final goal. He follows this way, not out of fear of punishment or out of hope of heaven. To him the Koran says: "Do as you like; Allah has forgiven you all." In the last stage of his development the believer obtains *Ieqan* (certainty) of faith. The *Shariat* becomes *Haqiqat* (reality). He then recognizes this reality as identical with his own being. He discovers that what he learned, as if it came from without, is nothing but the voice of his deepest being: he himself really becomes the way. Thus he can say: "I am the way." His will becomes one with that of his creator; he returns all that was given him with the words of the Koran: "In truth, my prayers, my sacrifice, my life and death are for the sake of Allah, creator and sustainer of the worlds" (6:163–164). This was contained in the vow he took when he pronounced the *Kalima* (the word or "parole"): "La ilaha illa Allah" (I profess that no one is worthy of adoration except Allah and that there is no object of love and desire except Allah). This is not yet the end of the journey. A new phase begins. What I have just described is called *Nirvana* by the Buddhist and "to lose oneself in God" by the Christian. The Muslim calls it *Fana* (to lose oneself in God).

This *Fana* can be achieved even in this life and leads to *Baqa* (life): "Do not think that those who were killed on the way to Allah are dead: they are in life" (3:170). When man has entered upon this life he will experience *Liqa* (the encounter), which is union with the creator, the source of life for us all.

This description of the various stages might give the impression that we need centuries to reach the final goal. And this would be so if this spiritual development were bound to time and space. But this is not the case. We need a turning point in our life. We do not need centuries to come to see that our only purpose is to strive toward the creator. When man realizes this, a revolution takes place within himself. This revolution makes it possible for us to make a journey of centuries within a few moments. The initiate who starts on the way toward union with God can go through various stages of his journey simultaneously. It will depend on inner disposition and purity of motive and resolution. This stage is reached from within. From outside no one can lift us onto that level. That is why the Muslim does not believe in a mediator who can bring about our redemption.

We are all seekers after the truth. May Allah grant us all to find the purpose for which we were created in this life. To Allah, creator and sustainer of the worlds, be all praise.

THE HINDU SCRIPTURES
Cyril Papali, O.C.D., Rome, Italy

All the great religions of the world boast of scriptures which they consider sacred and infallible. Hinduism is outstanding even in this respect, both for the antiquity and multiplicity of its sacred books, and for the extraordinary fidelity with which some of them have been preserved for thousands of years. These scriptures fall into two categories: the çruti (hearing) or revelation, and the smṛti (memory) or sacred tradition. It must be noted that this division into revelation and tradition does not correspond to the Christian scheme of Scripture and tradition, both of which are revelation. To the Hindu, only the çruti is revelation; the smṛti scriptures are works which the sages who received the above-mentioned revelation later composed of their own accord in confirmation of the revelation. The idea of inspiration in the Christian sense does not play any part here.

The çruti literature consists of the four Vedas while the smṛti is represented by a vast array of books of varying degrees of importance. In this short treatise we shall limit our attention to the former, as only they are sacred scriptures in the strictest sense, though a few of the smṛtis have in practice acquired an importance comparable with that of the Vedas.

The Four Vedas

The name is derived from the root "vid", meaning "to see", "to know", because the contents of these books are believed to have been seen by the sages. The four Vedas are: the Rik, the Sāma, the Yajus and the Adharva. By far the most important of them is the Rik-Veda, the next two being mainly derived from it. The Adharva, on the other hand, is different from the other three both in style and contents, and was universally accepted as a Veda only late in the 3rd century B.C.

Each of the Vedas consists of three distinct parts, corresponding to three important periods in the evolution of the Indo-Aryan religion prior to the Christian era. The first and the most venerable part of the Vedas, called Samhita (collection), consists of hymns composed between 1500 and 1000 B.C. It is among the earliest literary productions of mankind known to history, and is a work of no mean order. These hymns play an important part in the religious rites of the Hindus even today.

The Samhita is the *Upāsana-kāṇḍa* (worship section) of the Vedas.

Next comes the *Karma-kāṇḍa* (action section) consisting of a large number of liturgical treatises known as *Brāhmaṇas,* composed between 1000 and 800 B.C. They describe in the minutest detail the ceremonies to be followed in the performance of sacrifices and other religious services. Though animal sacrifices which hold a prominent place in this section have long since fallen into disuse, the sacramental system of the Hindus and the rest of the sacred rites still in use are based on this part of the Vedas.

Finally we have the *Jñāna-kāṇḍa* (wisdom section), which is also known as the *Vedānta* (the end of the Vedas). This is made up of those marvelous books, the *Upanishads,* the most important of which were composed between 800 and 300 B.C. They are the cream of Indo-Aryan speculation on God, the world and the soul. Their intuitions on the nature and attributes of God surpass anything that unaided human reason has ever attained. But speculation on the world and the soul, without the right notion of creation, was bound to prove disastrous, and the Upanishads in the main tend either to deny the reality of the world or to explain it on pantheistic lines. They determined once and for all the trend of philosophic speculation in India, and have even exercised a profound influence on some of the Western thinkers, beginning with Schopenhauer who treasured the Upanishads in his closet and often knelt before them in worship.

The Authority of the Vedas

Absolute faith in the Vedas is the prime requirement of a true Hindu. He has to accept them as *nitya* (eternal) and *apauruṣeya* (without a human author); one who refuses to do so is a heretic. Even great philosophers blindly accept the Vedas without ever questioning their claims to credence. Stranger still, there have been philosophers who denied God, but all the same maintained the authority of the Vedas. This attitude is unintelligible until we take into account the peculiar theories they hold regarding the Vedas.

In what sense are the Vedas eternal and infallible? To the ordinary Hindu and to those philosophers who believe in a personal God, the Vedas are eternal in the sense that they have always been in the mind of God, and infallible because revealed by him. But not so to the *Pūrva-Mīmāmsa,* the philosophic system expressly devised to interpret the Vedas. According to it, the Vedas subsist by themselves, objectively, in the form of *çabda* (word, logos) in the ethereal sphere, irrespective of whether there is a God or not. The Vedas are eternal self-subsisting truth. The sages in their ecstasy saw them and faithfully rendered them in human words, all of which correspond exactly to their eternal originals in sense and arrangement. Here, again, the question of who the sages were and whether they did in fact see the vision and record their findings correctly seems to have received little attention.

The Exegesis of the Vedas

This is the most remarkable achievement of the Mīmāmsa school, and the rules of interpretation perfected by Jaimini a couple of centuries before Christ have much in common with modern biblical exegesis. There is an important difference, however. The biblical scholar has to discover not only the literal meaning of the text considered in its entire context, but beyond it also the spiritual meaning the divine author has superimposed on it. The Vedic interpreter has only to determine the true meaning of the text studied in its context; there is no divine author behind it whose mind he has to explore. For the rest, the rules of interpreting words and sentences, parallel texts, apparent contradictions, etc., are in general of such universal and timeless value that they have been followed in the interpretation of other texts as well, particularly of the Hindu law books. We cannot go into further details here, though that would have been very interesting to Scripture experts. However, we must mention an important principle enunciated by Jaimini. There is in the Vedas a famous text that reads: *Svargakāmo yajeta* ("Desirous of heaven, let him sacrifice." This text is taken as the model of all Vedic injunctions: the word *svargakāmo* ("desirous of heaven") is to be understood in every Vedic precept, even if it is not mentioned, because the salvation of the soul is the principal motive (*pradhāna codana*) of all Vedic laws. If what appears to be a precept is irreconcilable with the desire of heaven, then it is not a precept but merely a statement. For example, it is also said in the Veda: "Hurt your enemy with the *syena* ceremony." Here, evidently, the desire of heaven cannot be fitted in. The text, therefore, is not a precept but a mere statement of what could be done by evil-minded people.

The Conservation of the Vedas

If the conservation of the Bible is to be attributed principally to a special providence of God, in the survival of the Vedas we have an example of human ingenuity and industry unparalleled elsewhere. Until writing was introduced about the 7th century B.C., the Vedas were transmitted by word of mouth. The principal task of the Brahmin caste was to study the Vedas by heart, pronounce them accurately and transmit them faithfully, and they were experts at it. Even now Hindus consider oral tradition the most worthy way of transmitting the Vedas. When writing was finally introduced, the Brahmins devised an intricate system of codification. It evolved in the following order. First appeared *Pada-pāṭha* (the verbal test) in which each word was written separately, avoiding thereby the transformations which sanskrit words undergo when they combine. Next came *Krama-pāṭha* (the gradual text) in which each word was repeated thus: aa.bb.cc., etc. The third step was *Kaṭa-pāṭha* (the woven text) in which each member of the previous formula is repeated thrice in direct-inverse-direct order: ab.ba.ab; bc.cb.bc; cd.dc.cd, etc. And finally, *Ghana-pāṭha* (the ponderous text), the formula for which is: ab.ba.abc.cba.abc; bc.cb.bcd.dcb.bcd, etc. By such means they rendered the text so solidly interlocked that changes and interpolations were all but impossible. To decode the text into intelligible language they also produced appropriate keys (*pratisakhya*), and then, as a final seal, they annexed to each manuscript an index minutely indicating the number of chapters, pages, lines in each page, and words and even syllables in each line. No wonder the Vedas have survived the attrition of twenty-five centuries in remarkably good shape.

------◆◀◉▶◆------

BUDDHISM AND THE TRIPIṬAKA
Bayu Watanabe, Tokyo, Japan

Before considering the relation between Buddhism as a religion and its sacred texts, we must first provide some historical information on the very special characteristics of these scriptures. We can then examine the role of the texts in the religion of today.

The scriptures of primitive Buddhism are called *Tripiṭaka* (three baskets). They are in fact composed of three collections of texts. (1) The *Sutras* (texts) reproduce the teaching of Gautama Buddha, the founder of Buddhism. (2) The *Vinaya* (discipline) is the monastic rule of the community founded by Buddha. Note the importance attached in the scriptures to the monastic rule; it shows that in the beginning Buddha's teaching was addressed chiefly to the religious "who retired from the world". In proportion as the laity, under the influence of the "Greater Vehicle", grew in importance, interest in the *Vinaya* inevitably decreased. (3) The *Abhidharma* (doctrinal treatise) aims at expounding the meaning of the Buddha's direct teaching, comprised in the *Sutras* and the *Vinaya* during the first centuries after his *Nirvana*. It formed a corpus of the doctrines of the "Lesser Vehicle". From the *Abhidharma* we can appreciate what a profound respect the followers of the Lesser Vehicle have attributed to Buddha's every word and phrase.

The followers of the Lesser Vehicle, who comprise the majority in several countries of Southeast Asia, take their stand on the tradition of the *Tripiṭaka* in Pali, an ancient Indian tongue.

Recently there has been a tendency to translate the scriptures into local languages (Cambodian, Singhalese, etc.), but their content is regarded as immutable. Hence certain problems arise regarding how prescriptions valid for the time and the land in which Buddha lived can be adapted to modern life.

Subsequently, the tendency of the Greater Vehicle to insist that illumination can be obtained by all men gave rise to the creation of a new sacred literature. These texts, although they introduce new doctrines and contradict the old, are attributed to Buddha himself. Rising above all the accidents of history and geography, they strive toward a universal formulation that is faithful to the spirit of Buddha. A particular trend of the Greater Vehicle in China, known as Zen, has even preached a certain rejection of the scriptures in order to attain personal illumination.

The spread of Buddhism outside India, its land of origin, came about chiefly through the propagation of the texts. A considerable effort, certainly unprecedented in the history of any other religion, was carried through to translate the texts so that they would be intelligible in Chinese and accurate in Tibetan. It was mainly the Buddhism of the Greater Vehicle in a Chinese translation which spread in China and Japan.

What is the attitude of Japanese Buddhists, who at present form the majority of the Japanese people, toward the scriptures?

The Buddhist canon in Chinese is enormous. To the *Tripiṭaka,* already mentioned, and in the texts of the Greater Vehicle, have been added numerous commentaries of many different tendencies. In the face of this multiplicity and diversity, Japanese Buddhism has split into about ten sects, each of which emphasizes one particular aspect of Buddhist doctrine. The founders of the sects chose these aspects in virtue of their religious experience and commented upon them. It is these texts and their commentaries, differing from sect to sect, which represent the scriptures for the Japanese Buddhists of today. Again we find ourselves up against the problem of how these texts, at least several centuries old, can be adapted to the upheavals of modern life.

There is now a movement in Japan for the translation of the

scriptures. On one hand, the effort is being made to translate into modern Japanese the original Sanskrit and Pali texts of primitive Buddhism. It means a return to the sources, so that by scientific means they may provide material for the devotion of the ordinary faithful. On the other hand, since the Chinese Buddhist translations and texts are written in a very technical and archaic language, an attempt is also being made to render these texts into modern Japanese and modern Korean. All these translations are provided with explanatory matter. It should be said that they still form a source of reference only for the educated Buddhists. In traditional circles, and for the ceremonies, people remain strictly faithful to the canonical texts in their Chinese version, which is almost always unintelligible to the masses.

Japanese Buddhists are therefore faced with the necessity of reconciling a sometimes rather formalistic fidelity to tradition with understanding of the Buddhist doctrine.

———◆◀◉▶◆———

SHINTO
Kiichi Numazawa, S.V.D., Nagoya, Japan

The name "Shinto", which means "way of the gods", appears for the first time in the Chronicle of Emperor Yomei (519–87) in *Nihonshoki*. Insofar as we can make out from the two oldest Japanese books—*Kojiki* (A.D. 712) and *Nihonshoki* (A.D. 720)—Shinto is a compilation of all the mythological religious views and customs which existed before Indian and Chinese ideas were introduced and which had been handed on from one generation to another since primitive times. The origins of Shinto are as old and varied as those of the Japanese people who come from a very mixed background. Yet, within this Shinto there are a few constant religious elements.

The God of the Heavens

Right at the beginning the *Kojiki* mentions three sexless, invisible divinities of the heavens. The first is called Amenominakanushi (the Lord of the exalted center of the heavens); the second, Takamimusubi (the high exalted begetter); the third, Kamimusubi (the divine exalted begetter). This curious threesome has tempted some commentators to see here some analogy with the Christian Trinity. There is also the view that Amenominakanushi is really the only and highest God of the heavens and that the other two are but personifications of his outward activities. Yet, it is precisely of this Amenominakanushi that we hear nothing in the whole mythology, while there are rich myths concerning the original ancestors—Izanagi and Izanami, Amaterasu, Susanowo and others—kept alive in the Japanese tradition. Insofar as Amenominakanushi is concerned, the sources tell us no more than that in the mental world of the author there existed a God of the heavens by this name and that he occupied the first place in the list of gods. He has no parents, no wife, no children. It is also curious that, from the earliest times, no sanctuary is known to be dedicated to him. The author of *Kojiki* and many other commentators say that he created heaven and earth. He is omnipresent and his worship is not tied to any particular place. So we have here a God of the heavens without myths and without cult.

The Cult of the Ancestors

Throughout Japanese mythology the most important part is played by Amaterasu as the ancestral divinity of the imperial stock and at the same time as the goddess of the sun. According to Japanese mythology the original ancestors said to each other before they begot Amaterasu: "We have already begot the land of Ohyashima [Japan] with its mountains, rivers, herbs and trees. Why should we not beget someone to be lord of this world?" And so they begot Amaterasu whom they then appointed Mistress of the world and of the land of Ohyashima. Since the original ancestors begot all gods at the same time as all objects and phenomena of nature, Amaterasu was deemed to be the highest of all divinities. This Amaterasu is said to have commissioned Ninigi, who started the line of emperors, as follows: "This land of the field of the fifteen hundred autumnal-fresh heads of bull-rushes [Japan] is the region over which my descendants will rule. Therefore, you, my grandchild, sovereign and illustrious, go forth and rule it" (*Nihonshoki*). Inasmuch as all the gods, begotten like Amaterasu from the same original ancestors, are linked with this goddess as their sister, all tribes, clans and families are related by blood relationship to Amaterasu and her descendants, the imperial family, and so constitute a kind of extensive family with this imperial family, the center of which lies primarily among all the sisters, Amaterasu, and her direct descendants, the imperial family. The tendency to group in this way all the mythological religious divinities and all historical tribes and clans into one unit is admittedly inspired by the political interests of the imperial dynasty. The real aim which inspired the composition of the two oldest books was precisely to show the divine origin and the political legitimacy of the imperial family as the rulers of people and country. The form in which the ancestors' cult is presented in both books can hardly be considered religion.

Nature Worship

Most gods incorporated in Japanese mythology and linked with mythological ancestors and heroes, including the sun goddess Amaterasu, were originally religious objects of popular belief. Most of these religious elements continued to remain alive for a long time in this popular belief. This old Japanese popular belief, before it had been influenced by the ancestors' cult in the form in which the two ancient books presented it, was in large measure a mixture of nature worship and animism. All the objects and phenomena of nature—the sun, the moon, the storm, the mountains, the rivers, several kinds of animals, plants, and so on—were worshiped as *Kami* (divinities). Often they were considered as *Kami* themselves, but it also happened that some of them were considered as inhabited by spirits and demons. One sentence in the ancient books says that formerly rocks and stones, trees and herbs spoke. Such *Kami* brought fear and misfortune to men according to their deserts, but they could also dispense favors when invoked and prayed to.

The Kami as Such

Apart from the religious elements mentioned one can also find traces of shamanistic and totemistic worship in the Shinto of those times. It may also be said that behind all this polytheism there lived the worship of a monotheistic deity. Above all, Amenominakanushi is the practically isolated highest God of the heavens, above the whole world of gods. In mythology he has no connection with any other god. He lived among the people under the name of "God of the heavens". On the other hand, Amaterasu often has the features of a highest divinity, particularly as venerated in the sanctuary of Ise. In general, when an ordinary Japanese stands before a sanctuary and prays, he usually does not think of a particular god with a particular name and a particular sanctuary, but simply invokes the *Kami,* and this is so even today. In this case the *Kami* is thought of as the supreme God; even though not explicitly put into words, it is implicitly felt. Most Japanese do not even know to whom the sanctuary is dedicated where they at that moment stand praying. They simply pray to the *Kami*.

THE USE OF THE BIBLE BY THE JEHOVAH'S WITNESSES
Jean Séguy, Boulogne-sur-Seine, France

Catholic authors, following on this point a common tendency of Protestant apologetics, often regard the Jehovah's Witnesses as a non-Christian religion. At best these are allowed the status of a new religion born on Protestant soil. The reasons given in support of this view can be reduced to two: (1) the Witnesses interpret the Bible in the light of the official books published by their leaders, instead of drawing their beliefs from direct study of the Bible; (2) they reject some beliefs which are central to the Christianity of the Bible: the divinity of Christ, the Trinity, the eternity of the pains of hell, etc. To this the Witnesses reply: "We believe everything that the Bible teaches. Our manuals (the books of the founder, C. T. Russell, and the publications of the group) present the content of the Bible in a systematic form. The particular beliefs we reject, which are traditional among the 'religionists', really contradict the scriptures and are of pagan origin."

This mutual contradiction brings us to the heart of the problem before us: the use made of the Bible by the Witnesses. From the purely social-historical point of view, neither of the two positions here summarized can be justified. They reflect opposed and irreconcilable principles of interpretation. We shall understand them only if we abandon the ground on which they stand. Here we need only to concentrate our attention on the position of the Witnesses.

Historically speaking, the Witnesses originated as a result of the opposition experienced by the adventist movements in the United States, in the last quarter of the 19th century, among a poorly educated class, hesitating between a popular doctrinal liberalism and a paradoxical attachment to the letter of Scripture. These last characteristics account for the use made of the Bible by the Witnesses.

The adventist movement, from which the Witnesses, while retaining their interest in eschatological speculations, very soon diverged, belongs to a particular form of German and Anglo-Saxon pietism. This may be called "prophetic pietism", and it is connected both with the German pietist movement and with the preaching of the exiled "prophets" of the Covennes in 18th-century England and Germany. The groups which are influenced by them insist both on eschatology and on the "spirit of prophecy".

This last expression means that the "last times"—the 18th and 19th centuries—are characterized by an "abundance of new light" on God's design. The "vessels" or mediators of this revelation, or these revelations, who are to enlighten believers in times of crisis, are "prophets", speaking with authority. Among the Seventh Day Adventists Mrs. Helen White is acknowledged as one of these "vessels". Candidates for admission to baptism in this group must declare that they acknowledge the spirit of prophecy as it is manifested in the foundress. The views of the Adventists are all, in effect, contained in Mrs. White's writings, which are mainly commentaries on the Bible.

Much the same has happened with the Witnesses, except that the fossilization of the charismatic phenomenon took place in a different way. Russell, their founder, claimed to have received the spirit of prophecy and to speak with authority. The books in which he commented on the Bible, and especially its apocalyptic and eschatological passages, form the basis of the Witnesses' teaching. But, being less flexible than Mrs. White, he put more emphasis on his interpretations than on the text he interpreted. He held his writings, however, to be "divinely authorized", not inspired. In this respect his case is similar to that of Mrs. White, and here, too, the Witnesses and the Seventh Day Adventists differ from Christian Scientists and the Mormons, for whom the writings of their founders (*Science and Health* and *The Book of Mormon* respectively) constitute a new revelation, added to the books of the Bible, just as Christianity supplemented the Old Testament with the New.

In strict logic the prophetic-pietist view of the Adventists and the Witnesses would require that prophecy should not be quenched until the parousia. Among the former it has been fossilized by the acceptance of the exclusive role of Mrs. White. With the latter, on the contrary, it continues. After Russell's death in 1916 his successor at the head of the movement, "Judge" Rutherford, undertook to correct those elements in his predecessor's teaching which had been falsified by events—for ex-

ample, the destruction of the "Gentiles" in 1914. Little by little
he set aside Russell's works, and his own became the basis of the
group's teaching. Since Rutherford's death in 1942, and the
accession of Nathan H. Knorr as head of the organization, the
books of interpretation used by the Witnesses as obligatory standards of reference have been written by a group of leaders appointed for this task. The spirit of prophecy, at first personal,
has become collective, or rather it is now incarnate in the group's
bureaucratic aristocracy. This change is itself the result of a new
reading of the scriptures. Russell in fact asserted himself to be
the "faithful and wise servant" of Matthew 24, 45–47. Rutherford was the first to interpret this singular as a plural, in order,
incidentally, to justify his substitution of his own views for Russell's.

All this takes us very far from the constantly repeated assertion
of the Witnesses that they hold to the Bible alone as the basis of
their belief. With them, Scripture is given an interpretation by
one man, or several men, in the framework of a more general
tradition, which is at once traditional content and the transmis-
sion and adaptation of that content. As to this process the ordinary Witnesses are extremely reserved, and there are several
reasons for this. In the first place they are, by and large, almost
entirely ignorant of the history of their movement. Secondly,
they nearly always see in the manuals of their group nothing
but an obvious commentary on the Bible, never suspecting that
for equally sound reasons it could be interpreted otherwise in
all good faith. Finally, all the posts in the movement are elective,
so that all the members share in some way, however remotely,
in the elaboration of the "truth". Each of them, by procuration,
is a messianic figure. But nothing of this is admitted in their
public teaching. Nonetheless, alongside their claim to hold to
the Bible alone is their actual practice, in which the manuals
published at Brooklyn play a more important part than Holy
Scripture, not only in their worship but in their study circles and
their sale of literature. But this seems to escape the notice of

the rank-and-file Witness. At the summit, moreover, they are convinced that only the interpretation provided by the officials is "divinely authorized".

From this point the theologians can take up the dialogue of confrontation outlined at the beginning of these pages. Two views of Christianity face each other, which in the present state of affairs are not likely to be reconciled.*

MORMON VIEW OF THE BOOK OF MORMON
Hugh Nibley, Provo, Utah

The first step in what the Mormons consider "The Restoration of the Gospel in the Dispensation of the Fullness of Times" was the coming forth of the Book of Mormon. More than anything else this fixed the unique status of the new religion, of which Eduard Meyer wrote: "Mormonism . . . is not just another of those innumerable new sects, but a new religion of revelation (*Offenbarungsreligion*)." [1] The Latter-Day Saints "believe the Book of Mormon to be the Word of God" in exactly the same sense as the Bible (Article of Faith No. 8)—a proposition which has caused great offense to many Christians and led to long and severe persecutions, the Book of Mormon being the principal object of attack.

However, the book does not take the place of the Bible in Mormonism. But just as the New Testament clarified the long misunderstood message of the Old, so the Book of Mormon is

* For a more complete study, besides the movement's own literature, studies on its history and theology will be found in A. Hoekema's *The Four Major Cults* (Grand Rapids, Michigan, 1963) which I feel is the best from the theological point of view. From a sociological aspect, see H. H. Stroup, *The Jehovah's Witnesses* (New York, 1945).

[1] E. Meyer, *Ursprung und Geschichte der Mormonen* (Halle, 1912), p. 1.

held to reiterate the messages of both Testaments in a way that restores their full meaning. Its professed mission, as announced on its title page, is "to show unto the remnant of the House of Israel how great things the Lord hath done for their fathers; and that they may know the covenants of the Lord, that they are not cast off forever; and also to the convincing of the Jew and Gentile that Jesus is the Christ, the eternal God, manifesting himself unto all nations". Until recently, most Mormons have not been zealous in the study of the book, considering it on the whole a strange and alien document with little relationship to modern life. Its peculiar effectiveness has indeed been as a messenger (it was brought by an angel) to the world at large.

The Book of Mormon professes to present in highly abridged form the history of a peculiar civilization, transplanted from the Old World to the New around 600 B.C. Of complex cultural background and mixed racial stock, the society endured only a thousand years, of which period the Book of Mormon contains an unbroken account, taken supposedly from records kept almost entirely by the leaders of a minority religious group. The first of the line was Lehi, who with his family and some others fled from Jerusalem to the desert to live the law in its purity and prepare for the coming Messiah. Commanded by God after much wandering to cross the seas, the community reached the New World and there broke up, only a minority choosing to continue the ways of the pious sectaries of the desert. Lehi's descendants in time met and mingled with yet other migrants from the Old World, and indeed for almost 500 years they had, unawares, as their northern neighbors warlike hunting tribes which, according to the Book of Mormon, had come from Asia thousands of years before. The racial and cultural picture of the Book of Mormon is anything but the oversimplified thing its critics have made it out to be. For the Mormons, the Book of Mormon contains "the fullness of the Gospel". Six hundred years of its history transpire before the coming of Christ, and four hundred after that. In the earlier period the faithful minority formed a church of anticipation, their charismatic leaders "teaching the law of Moses, and the intent for which it was given; persuading them to look forward unto the Messiah, and believe in him to come as though he already was". There are extensive quotations from the Old Testament prophets, especially Isaiah, with remarkable variant readings, and much that is reminiscent in language and imagery of early Jewish apocryphal writings. The boldest part of the Book of Mormon is the detailed account of the visit of Jesus Christ to his "other sheep" in the New World after the resurrection, including his instructions and commandments to the new Church. This episode closely parallels certain sections of early Christian apocrypha dealing with post-resurrectional teachings of the Lord to his disciples in Galilee and on the Mount of Olives, although none of these sources was available in Joseph Smith's day.

The historical parts of the Book of Mormon bear witness to its good faith, which never claims for it any sort of immunity, religious or otherwise, from the most searching scientific and scholarly criticism. Lack of comparative historical documents is offset by an abundance of cultural data: over 200 non-biblical Hebrew and Egyptian names offer ample material to the philologist, and a wealth of technical detail invites critical examination, thanks to precise descriptions of such things as the life of a family wandering in the Arabian desert, a great earthquake, the ancient craft of olive-culture, a major war in all its phases, the ways of the early desert sectaries, the state of the world during a protohistoric Völkerwanderung, etc.

Along with cultural-historical particulars the religious message of the book is richly interspersed with peculiar expressions, legends, traditions, and customs supposedly derived from the Old World, which may today be checked against ancient sources. Thus it describes certain practices of arrow-divination, an odd custom of treading on garments, a coronation ceremony (in great detail), the evils of the archaic matriarchy, peculiar ways of keeping and transmitting sacred records, the intricacies of an ingenious monetary system, and the like.

Of particular interest to Latter-Day Saints are the prophetic parts of the Book of Mormon, which seem to depict the present state of the world most convincingly. The last 140 years have borne out exactly what the book foretold would be its own reception and influence in the world, and its predictions for the Mormons, the Jews and the other remnants of scattered Israel (among which are included the American Indians) seem to be on the way to fulfillment. The Book of Mormon allows an ample time-scale for the realization of its prophecies, according to which the deepening perplexities of the nations, when "the Lord God shall cause a great division among the people", shall lead to worldwide destructions by fire, for "blood, and fire, and vapor of smoke must come; and it must needs be upon the face of this earth". After this the survivors (for this is not to be the end of the world) shall have learned enough to coexist peaceably "for the space of many years", when "all nations, kindreds, tongues and people shall dwell safely in the Holy One of Israel if it so be that they will repent".

The Book of Mormon is the history of a polarized world in which two irreconcilable ideologies confronted each other, and is addressed explicitly to our own age, faced by the same predicament and the same impending threat of destruction. It is a call to faith and repentance couched in the language of history and prophecy, but above all it is a witness to God's concern for all his children, and to the intimate proximity of Jesus Christ to all who will receive him.

BIOGRAPHICAL NOTES

JOHN L. MCKENZIE, S.J.: Born in 1910 in Indiana, U.S.A., he was ordained in 1939. He studied at Xavier University in Cincinnati, the University of St. Louis and at Weston College, where he obtained his degree in arts and a doctorate in theology. He has been professor of Old Testament studies at the University of Notre Dame, Indiana, since 1965.

FRANÇOIS DREYFUS, O.P.: Born in France in 1918, he studied at the Saulchoir, the Ecole Polytechnique and the Biblical College in Jerusalem. An engineer, he is also a doctor of theology and of Scripture, and he holds the posts of professor of Scripture and head of theological studies at the Saulchoir. He contributes to the *Revue des Sciences Philosophiques et Théologiques* and to *Vie Spirituelle*.

FRANCO FESTORAZZI: Born in Italy in 1928, he was ordained in 1952. He studied at the Gregorian and at the Biblical Institute in Rome, gaining his licentiate in Scripture. He teaches Scripture at the major seminary in Como, Italy, and is presently engaged in writing his doctoral thesis on this subject. He has published *La Bible et le probléme des origines* (Brescia, 1966) and is a contributor to *Rivista Biblica* and *Scuola Cattolica*.

JACOBUS VINK, O.P.: Born in Holland in 1928, he was ordained in 1963. He received his doctorate in theology *cum laude* in 1967, and in that same year he became professor of Scripture at the Dominican House of Studies in Nijmegen. He is the author of *Leviticus, uit de grondtekst vertaald en uitgelegd* (Roermond, 1962), and has contributed to *Tijdschrift voor Theologie*.

ELPIDIUS PAX, O.F.M.: Born in Germany in 1912, he was ordained in 1950. He studied at the universities of Breslau, Berlin and Munich, and also at the Biblical Institute in Rome. He gained his licentiate in Scripture and doctorates in philosophy and theology, and since 1960 has been professor of Old Testament studies and biblical theology at the Atheneum Antoniano in Jerusalem, where he has also been rector since 1963. He is the author of *Epiphaneia* (Heidelberg 1955).

HEINRICH GROSS: Born in Bonn in 1916, he was ordained in 1947. He studied at the College of Philosophy and Theology at Trier, at Bonn University, and at the Biblical Institute in Rome. He gained his licentiate in Scripture and a doctorate in theology in 1951, and is now professor of Old Testament studies in the Trier theological faculty. He is the author of *L'idée de paix mondiale perpétuelle et universelle dans l'Orient ancien et l'Ancien Testament* (Trier, 1956), and is a contributor to the five-volume symposium *Mysterium Salutis*.

SALVADOR MUÑOZ IGLESIAS: Born in Madrid in 1917, he was ordained in 1940. He studied at the Gregorian and Biblical Institute in Rome. He gained his licentiate *ad lauream* in Scripture and his doctorate in theology (1947). He is professor of Scripture at Madrid's major seminary, director of the biblical department of the Francisco Suarez Institute, and editor of the review *Estudios Bíblicos*. Among his published works are *Doctrina Pontificia, I—Documentos Bíblicos* (Madrid, 1955) and *Introducción a la lectura del A.T.* (Madrid, 1965).

HILAIRE DUESBERG, O.S.B.: Born in Belgium in 1888, he was ordained in 1914. He studied at San Anselmo and the Angelicum in Rome and at the Biblical College in Jerusalem. He was dean of Oriental studies at Fribourg University from 1942 to 1957. Among his published works are *Les valeurs chrétiennes de l'A.T.* (1948) and *Aspects bibliques du mystére de la messe* (1962). He is secretary of and a contributor to *Bible et Vie chrétienne*.

JOSEPH COPPENS: Born in 1896 in Belgium, he was ordained in 1920, receiving a doctorate in theology. He has been professor of Old Testament exegesis at Louvain since 1927, and is a member and ex-president of the Belgian Royal Academy, honorary member of the British Society for Old Testament Studies, editor of the series *Recherches Bibliques,* and member of the editorial committee of *Ephemerides Theologicae Lovanienses*. Foremost among his numerous publications is *La Connaissance du bien et du mal et le péché du paradis* (Louvain, 1948).

RABBI ARTHUR GILBERT: Born in 1926, in Philadelphia, he earned a degree in letters in 1947 at New York University, and in Hebrew and rabbinical studies at the Jewish Institute of Religion. From 1951 to 1954 he pursued further studies in psychology and psychoanalysis. In his post as director of the National Department of Interreligious Cooperation, he worked for better relations between the Jewish community and Protestants, Catholics and Moslems. Since 1965 he has been director of the National Department of Interreligious Curriculum Research and of the Anti-Defamation League of B'nai B'rith. Among his published works are *The Jews in Christian America* (1966), *Currents and Trends in Contemporary Jewish Thought* (1966), *Religion and the Public Order* (1964), and many contributions to reviews such as *Editorial Board, Reconstructionist* and the *Journal of Ecumenical Studies*. Scheduled for publication in the near future is a study entitled *The Vatican Council and the Jews*.

GHULAM BASHIR: A Pakistani, he was born in India in 1918. He studied at the University of the Punjab and Ahmadiyyah College. He is imam of the Moslem community in the Netherlands, where he also teaches Urdu at Leyden University. He is editor of the monthly Moslem review published in Holland, *Al-Fariq*, and author of various articles concerning Christianity and Mohammedanism, notably on the Ahmadiyyan movement.

CYRIL PAPALI, O.C.D.: Born in 1902 in India, he was ordained in 1931. He studied in India at the Pontifical Seminary of Alwaye. He was a Vatican Council II *peritus* and is a member of the post-conciliar commission, advisor to the Secretariat for Non-Christian Religions, member of the Commission for the Reform of Ecclesiastical Studies, and professor of Indology and missionary methodology at the Urbaniana and Teresianum in Rome. He is the author of the two-volume *Hinduismus* (Rome, 1953, 1960).

BAYA WATANABE: Born in Japan in 1893, he is a priest of the Soto-Shû branch of Zen Buddhism. He gained his doctorate in literature at the University of Kyoto, Japan, and is a member of the executive committee of the Japanese Association for Religious Studies. He lectures on Buddhism at the Nîhon University in Tokyo. Among his published works are *History of Thoughts in Mahâyâna Buddhism* (Tokyo, 1948), and *Religions in Japan Today* (Tokyo, 1950).

KIICHI NUMAZAWA, S.V.D.: Born in Japan in 1907, he was ordained in 1938. He studied at Sophia University in Tokyo and the Seminary of St. Augustine in Germany, at the Gregorian, and at the University of Fribourg, Switzerland, receiving his doctorate in philosophy in 1942. He is professor of ethnology at Nanzan University in Japan, of which he is also president. Among his writings is an important contribution on the religions of Japan to *Christus und die Religionen der Erde* (Vienna, 1951).

JEAN SÉGUY: Born in France in 1925, he studied at the Sorbonne, gaining a degree in literature and his doctorate in the science of religions (1965). He is head of the National Committee of Scientific Research (C.M.R.S.), and chairman of the School of Higher Studies at the Sorbonne since 1960. He is the author of *Les Sectes protestantes dans la France contemporaine* (Paris, 1956) and contributes to *Archives de sociologie des Religions* and *Internationales Jahrbuch für Religionssoziologie*.

HUGH NIBLEY: A Mormon, he was born in 1910 at Portland, Oregon. He studied at the universities of California and Chicago. He gained his degree in arts and a doctorate in philosophy, and since 1947 has been professor of history and religion at Brigham Young University, Utah. He is the author of *The World and the Prophets* (Salt Lake City, 1954 & 1965).

Subject Index to CONCILIUM (Volumes 21-30)